C Mytnology

Amazing Tales and Stories of Celtic Gods

(The Complete Guide to Learn All About the Celtic Heroes)

Rosie Renaud

Published By **John Kembrey**

Rosie Renaud

All Rights Reserved

Celtic Mythology: Amazing Tales and Stories of Celtic Gods (The Complete Guide to Learn All About the Celtic Heroes)

ISBN 978-1-77485-612-3

Legal & Disclaimer

information provided by this guide. This disclaimer applies to any damages or injury caused by the use and application, whether directly or indirectly, of any advice or information presented, whether for breach of contract, tort, negligence, personal injury, criminal intent, or under any other cause of action.

You agree to accept all risks of using the information presented inside this book. You need to consult a professional medical practitioner in order to ensure you are both able and healthy enough to participate in this program.

Table Of Contents

Introduction

Celtic Mythology has arguable captured the imagination of the western world more than any other cultural mythology except that of Greece and Rome. It is here that we learn of the tales of mythic monsters, great chivalric heroes, magicians, and fairy lands. Due to the vast and varied history of the Celtic people, however, it is difficult to narrow Celtic Mythology into a nice neat formula. It is especially difficult to cover it in a way that does the subject justice in such a short time period. Therefore, we will be addressing Celtic Mythology in two parts. This week we will discuss the general background of Celtic culture and the most famous of all heroic tales associated with the Celts--King Arthur. Next week we will dive into the remaining mythic themes (gods and goddess, creation, nature...etc).

Chapter 1: Celtic History

1.   La Tene Culture

The Celts are traced by scholars to the people of the La Tène Culture, which developed during the Iron Age from the previous Hallstatt Culture, in an original area extended between southern Germany, eastern France, and northern Switzerland, where there was a continuous cultural evolution.

To the early 13th-century urnfield culture BC, followed at the beginning of the eighth century BC, was the Hallstatt Culture, with an agricultural base but dominated by a class of warriors, with a commercial network toward Greeks, Scythians, and Etruscans. From this Central-Western European civilization, around the fifth century BC, Celtic culture developed. The various populations had a cultural and linguistic unity, but not a political one. In fact, they were made up of tribes of which the most important were: the Britons (British Isles), the Celtiberians (Iberian

Peninsula), the Pannonians (Pannonia), the Galatians (Anatolia), and the Gauls (Gauls).

The Celts were therefore neither a people nor a race, but a set of Indo-European peoples that expanded over a vast area of Europe, from the British Isles to the Danube and the Iberian, Italic, and Anatolian peninsulas. Caesar, Herodotus, Livy, Polybius, Tacitus, and others have narrated about them. They were an essentially nomadic population and, therefore, dedicated to raising livestock, in particular cows, sheep, and goats, from which they obtained meat, milk, and wool.

The most important groups were the Britons, the Gauls, the Pannonians, the Celtiberians, and the Galatians, settled respectively in the British Isles, Gaul, Pannonia, Iberia, and Anatolia. The Gauls in turn, constituted various groups, including the Belgians, the Helvetians, at the eastern end of Gaul, and the Cisalpine Gauls of northern Italy.

The expansion in the Iberian Peninsula and the French Atlantic coasts dates back to the eighth to seventh centuries BC. Later, in the

La Tène culture, they reached the English Channel, the mouth of the Rhine, present-day northwestern Germany, and the British Isles; then they went to Bohemia, Hungary, Austria, northern Italy, partly central Italy (early fourth century), and the Balkan Peninsula. In the third century, the group of Galatians passed from Thrace to Anatolia, and the Senonian Gauls in central Italy, through the supremacy of arms.

2.   The Tribes

Dislocation of the Gallic tribes before the conquest of Gaius Julius Caesar in 59 BC:

Allobrogi - Gaul between the Rhone river and Lake Geneva

Ambiani - Of Belgian Gaul

Ambibari - Of the Armorican people

Ambiliati - South of the Loire

Ambivareti - in the Aedui region

Andecavi or Andi - North of the lower course of the Loire

Aquitani - A mixture of Celts and Iberians from southwestern France

Arverni - Central Gaul, with King Vercingetorix

Atrebati - Of Belgian Gaul

Aulerci Cenomani - From Gallia Cisalpina, then also Lombardy and Veneto

Aulerci Eburovici - Normandy

Aulerci Diablinti - From Gallia Lugdunensis

Ausci - Aquitaine

Baiocassi - Lugdunense Gaul

Bellovaci - Northeastern Belgian Gaul

Betasii - In the Ardennes

Bigerrioni - Aquitaine

Biturigi - Bourges

Blannovi - In the Aedui region

Boi - Aquitaine

Cadurci - Close to the Arverni

Caleti - Close to the Armoricans (Belgians)

Carnuti - Chartres; they had the greatest power among the Celts

Catalauni - Châlons-en-Champagne

Caturigi - In the Cottian Alps

Ceutroni - In the Graian Alps

Cocosati - Aquitaine

Coriosolites - From the Côtes-du-Nord

Edui - Bibracte

Eleuteti - Close to the Arverni

Elvi - Bordered to the north with Narbonne Gaul

Elusati - Aquitaine

Elvezi - La Tene

Garonni - Aquitaine

Gabali - Bordered to the northwest with Narbonne Gaul

Gati - Aquitaine

Graioceli - Moncenisio area

Lemovici - Limoges

Lessovi - Lisieux of Normandy

Leuci - Between the Vosges and the Marne valley

Lingoni - Between the Seine and the Marne

Mandubi - Transalpine Gaul

Mediomatrixes - Metz

Meduli - Medoc

Meldi - Meaux

Menapi - Cassel

Morini - Boulogne-sur-Mer

Namneti - Nantes

Nantuati - Martigny

Nervi - Bavay

Nitiobrogi - Bordered to the northwest with Narbonne Gaul

Osisms - Of the Armorican Celts

Parisi - Paris

Petrocori - Périgueux, in Périgord

Pictoni - Poitiers

Ptiani - Aquitaine

Raurici - Basel

Redoni - Rennes

Remi - Reims

Ruthenians - Bordered to the northwest with Narbonne Gaul

Santoni - Saintes

Seduni - Martigny area

Segusiavi - Loire area

Senoni - Gaul-transalpine east of Orléans

Sequani - Besançon

Sibuzati - Aquitaine

Soziati - Aquitaine

Suessioni - Soissons

Tarbelli - Aquitaine

Tarusati - Aquitaine

Toulouse - Toulouse

Trier, Treveri - Trier

Tricassi - Troyes

Tungri - Tongeren

Turoni - Tours

Unelli - Normandy

Vangioni - Worms

Veliocassi - Rouen

Vellavi - Ruessium, in the Haute-Loire

Veneti - Vannes in Brittany

Veragri - Near Martigny

Viducassi - Vieux

Viromandui - Vermandois

Vocals - Aquitaine

Voconzi - Vaison-la-Romaine

Arecomic Volci - Gallia Narbonense

England, Ireland, Scotland, and Wales - Roman Britain and Celtic native tribes

Ancaliti - Hampshire and Wiltshire, England

Attacotti - Scotland or Ireland

Atrebati - Hampshire and Berkshire, England

Autini - Ireland

Belgians - Wiltshire and Hampshire, England

Bibroci - Berkshire, England

Brigands - Northern England, Ireland

Cereni - England

Caledoni - Scotland

Cantiaci - Kent, England

Carnonaci - West Scottish Highlands

Carvezi - Cumberland, England

Cassi - England

Catuvellauni - Hertfordshire, England

Cauci - Ireland

Corieltauvi - Leicestershire

Coriondi - Ireland

Corionotozi - Northumberland, England

Cornovi - Caithness, Cheshire, and Cornwall in England

Creons - Argyllshire

Damnoni - Strathclyde, England

Darini - Ireland

Deceangli - Flintshire

Decanzi - England

Demezi - Wales

Dobunni - Gloucestershire

Dumnoni - Devon, England

Durotrigi - Dorset, England

Eblani - Ireland

Epidi - Kintyre, England

Gangani - Ireland and the Lleyn Peninsula

Erpeditani - Ireland

Iberni - Ireland

Iceni - East Anglia, England

Lugi - England

Magnazi - Ireland

Manapi - Ireland

Novanzi - Galloway, England

Ordovici - Gwynedd, Wales

Parisi - East Riding, England

Regnensi - Sussex, England

Robogdi - Ireland

Segonziaci - England

Selgovi - Tweed, England

Setanzi - Lancashire, England

Torpedoes - Wales

Smerzi - England

Tassali - Aberdeenshire

Trinovanti - England

Vacomagi - England

Velabri - Ireland

Veniconi - England

Vennicni - Ireland

Vodie - Ireland

Votadini - Lothian

Cisalpine Gaul 391-192 BC

Boi - Emilia

Meat - Carnia

Galli Cenomani - Brescia

Galli Anari - Oltrepò Pavese

Gesati - Gallic mercenaries from the Rhone

Graioceli - Moncenisio and Lanzo Valleys

Insubri - Insubria

Lingoni - Ferrara, Lower Romagna

Salassi - Valle d'Aosta and Canavese

Senoni - From Romagna to the Ancona area

Taurini - Turin

Vertamocori - Novara

Central Europe - The Illyrian and Celtic populations

Anartii - Hungary

Arabiati - Illyria

Boi - Czech Republic, Slovakia, Hungary, and Germany

Cotini - Slovakia

Eravisci - Hungary

Ercuniati - Illyria

Osii - Slovakia

Scordisci - Croatia, Serbia

Taurisci - Noricus

Asia Minor (Turkey)

Galati: Volci Tectosagi, Tolostobogi, Trocmi

3.   The Costumes

Caesar calls unfortified villages vici and Celtic strongholds oppidum. The Celts, on the other hand, indicated with the term dunum the fortress and with nemeton a sacred place. Especially in Gaul, their cities had very thick walls. They lived mainly in wooden huts, circular or rectangular, and in villages. With the influence of the Etruscans and Greeks, they built stone houses with small rooms. They loved to live outdoors, under the oaks, considered sacred, where sacred rites and processes were held.

It was a tribal society, with villages that had an average of 25 inhabitants, and with a village chief who led the male warriors. In this society, now already distant in the time of Caesar from the matriarchal and magical one which is talked about in the various sagas, such as that of King Arthur, which seems to draw on myths of 1200 BC, gradually modified with the advent of the Christian religion, which disqualified in a stroke only women, children, priestesses, foresight, the Great Mother, the concept of death and magic.

In the patriarchal Celtic society, there were only men or men capable of fighting. Everything else, including wives and children, could be sacrificed, as seen in the battle of Alesia.

Being a warrior people, the Celts used splendid plumed helmets and sometimes armor, such as medieval ones, but they almost always fought naked. In battle, they colored their faces and, after having danced to reach the right momentum, threw themselves naked at the enemy, screaming. They preferred the melee and the first assault. For this reason, they struck with their swords, making cuts, which never proved to be fatal blows. The Celtic sword was, in fact, short and used as a cutting weapon.

Polybius says their little swords bent after the first blows. This was one of the reasons why they lost against the Romans, who instead used the sword and spears, hitting with deadly blows and avoiding the melee.

The shields, then, well finished and engraved, were small compared to the body, again because the Celts trusted in the impetus of the assault. The Romans had long shields; this was also a reason for the Celtic defeat.

The Celtic armies were not well organized and their war tactics were based mainly on war fury. Later, longer ones were forged, all inlaid and adorned with stones, but only after 500 AD.

The only Celtic king who understood that, in battle, it was necessary to use a strategy in addition to fury was the rooster Vercingetorix, who, using the "scorched earth" tactic, undermined the supplies of the Romans, obtaining some success. In particular, he understood that if he accepted direct confrontation with the Romans, he would lose.

The basic difference between them and the Romans is that while the Celts, like any tribal people, had to get excited with drums and drugs or alcohol to launch into war, for the Romans it was enough to receive an order and will. They were used to controlling their emotions, to obeying and leaving, as they were well aware that only organization and obedience could give them the victory over the barbarians.

They loved to shave their faces and comb their blond hair upwards, hardening it with chalk.

As for burials, they first used the tumulus tombs, typical of the Indo-European culture, and then the inmentation.

4.   The Capacites

They were experts in the art of weaving and dyeing and in the processing of minerals, especially iron. They introduced brass and, for a long time, worked with smithsonite, a particular mineral that replaces zinc. They were very familiar with the various casting techniques.

They were skilled in firing glass, both white and colored, in the use of enamel, and in the processing of amber. These practices were perfected during the transition from Hallstatt to Latenian culture.

In the maritime areas, they developed a skillful navigational ability. They possessed stronger ships than Roman ones, made of oak, with leather sails—ships that the Romans successfully copied.

They loved music very much, especially with the harp, which was used to celebrate sacred rites, in view of a war to set the spirits on fire, and to tell the deeds of heroes through ballads. For the Celts, fame was everything, especially because being remembered was considered a kind of immortality.

They traded and worked salt, in Celtic hal. In fact, many cities in the salt area have this term as an initial suffix.

They preferred the use of barrels to that of amphorae, and it seems they were the ones who invented the barrels. They were very fond of wine, but they also made beer.

5.   The Celtibers

The Celts who settled in the Iberian Peninsula were indicated, since ancient times, with the name of Celtiberi. The term has long been understood as a symptom of a hybridization between Celtic groups and Iberian groups, as indicated in antiquity by Diodorus Siculus, Appian, Martial, and

Strabo, who specified how the Celts were the dominant group. Among modern scholars, this interpretation has been supported by Johann Kaspar Zeuss. More recently, however, the hypothesis of a mixed population has been progressively discarded, and the term Celtiberi simply indicates the Celts who settled in Iberia.

The central nucleus of the Celtiberian settlement corresponds to an area of present-day central Spain, between the regions of Castile, Aragon, and La Rioja and between the middle basin of the Ebro and the upper course of the Tagus. The penetration in this area dates back to the eighth to seventh centuries BC. At a later time, the Celtiberians expanded southwards (in present-day Andalusia) and northwest, until they reached the Atlantic coasts of the peninsula (Galicia).

In the second century BC, the Celtiberians were subdued by Rome through a series of military campaigns, the Celtiberian Wars. The capitulation was marked by the fall of their last stronghold, Numantia, conquered in 133 BC by Publio Cornelio Scipione

Emiliano. From that moment on, the Celtibers, like all the other populations of the Iberian Peninsula, underwent an intense process of Latinization, dissolving as an autonomous people.

6.   The Gauls

Gauls was the name with which the Romans indicated the Celts who inhabited the region of the Gauls. From the original area of the La Tène culture, the Celts expanded toward the Atlantic coasts and along the course of the Rhine between the eighth and fifth centuries BC; later, starting from approximately 400 BC, they penetrated today's northern Italy. They continued to push south, so much so that in 390 BC, according to tradition, or more likely in 386 BC, the Senoni tribe led by Brenno sacked Rome itself, finally settling on the middle Adriatic side (Piceno).

The populations of Cisalpine Gaul 391-192 BC. Like all Celtic peoples, the Gauls were divided into numerous tribes, which in only rare cases were able to unite to face a common enemy, such as when, in 52 BC, numerous tribes led by Vercingetorix rebelled against the Caesarian conquest of Gaul. Among the Gallic populations, some groups of tribes were united by their own shared sub-identity: the Belgians, settled between the Channel and the Rhine and variously mixed with Germanic elements; the Helvetians, located in the upper Rhine and upper Danube areas and in contact with the Reti; the Aquitans, between the Garonne and the Pyrenees, mixed with Paleo-Basque peoples; and the Cisalpine Gauls, all the tribes that entered Cisalpine Gaul, on this side of the Alps. Among the populations of the central region of Gaul, Caesar attests that at the time of his campaigns, two factions were distinguished, headed respectively by the Aedui, traditionally from the second century BC, and by the Sequani, the latter soon ousted by the Remi.

The subjugation of the Gauls to Rome started in the third century BC: A series of military initiatives against the Cisalpine Gauls led to their complete submission, attested to by the creation of the province of Cisalpine Gaul around 90 BC. At that date in the once Celtic territory, there were already numerous Roman presences, in the form of municipalities and, above all, colonies. The conquest of transalpine Gaul began around 125-121 BC, with the occupation of the entire Mediterranean belt between the Ligurian Alps and the Pyrenees, subsequently constituted in the province of Gallia Narbonense. Northern Gaul came under the dominion of Rome following the campaigns conducted by Caesar between 58 and 50 BC.

Due above all to the testimony given by Caesar in his De bello Gallico, the Gallic civilization is by far the best known among those developed by the Celts in antiquity, even if the observations of the Roman statesman are likely to be extended—at least in general terms—to all the Celtic peoples. Cesare describes Gallic society as divided into family groups and divided into three classes: that of the producers, made up of farmers with formal rights, but politically subjected to the ruling classes; that of the warriors, holders of political rights, to whom the exercise of military functions was entrusted; and that of the druids, priests, magistrates and custodians of the culture, traditions, and collective identity of a people fragmented into numerous tribes.

7.   The Britons

Celtic populations reached Great Britain, crossing the Channel, in the eighth to sixth centuries BC. From present-day southern England, they later expanded rapidly north, colonizing the whole of Great Britain and Ireland, although pre-Indo-European Picts have long survived in present-day Scotland. Caesar attests to the close ties, not only cultural but also economic and political, between the Britons and the Gauls: The dominions of Diviziaco, for example, extended on both sides of the Channel and on the island escaped exiles from Gaul, which in turn he obtained, in case of need, military aid from Britain. A first Roman expedition, led by Caesar himself in 55 BC, did not involve an immediate subjugation of the Britons. This was completed about a century later, in 43 AD, by the emperor Claudius.

The Romans occupied the area of present-day England and Wales, erecting fortified limes to the north: Hadrian's Wall (122), later moved farther north (Antoninus Wall, 142). Beyond the limes (in present-day Scotland and Ireland), both British tribes and the Picts remained.

The Latinization of the Celtic tribes subject to Rome was intense, but less than that suffered by the Gauls and the Celtibers: At the end of the Roman control of Great Britain (late fourth to early fifth centuries), the ethnic and linguistic identity of the Celts was still alive, and also survived, for a long time, the subsequent Germanic invasions. From the fusion of the three elements— Celtic, Latin, and Germanic—the modern populations of Great Britain and Ireland were formed during the early Middle Ages. The only direct heirs of the ancient Celts are those of the British Isles, preserving the linguistic tradition in the two branches, Goidelic and Brythonic.

8. Pannoni

The process of expansion of the Celts toward the east, starting from the original cradle of the La Tène culture, is historically much less attested to than that which occurred toward the Gauls. However, it is believed that the penetration into that region of central Europe later identified with the name of Pannonia dates back to the early fourth century BC. In that area, on the middle course of the Danube, the Celts came into contact with the Illyrian tribes already present; in part, they intermingled with them and in part, they remained separated into autonomous groups, ethnically and linguistically homogeneous.

That of the Pannoni is the branch of the Celtic family on which the testimonies are scarce and uncertain; nothing remains of their language (certainly, a variety of continental Celtic languages), except perhaps for some isolated element which served as a substratum for the languages that later developed in that region. Among the Celtic tribes present in Pannonia, that of the Boi stands out—probably the eastern branch of a tribe also present in Gaul and penetrated into central Europe at a later time, perhaps in 50 BC. To them, we owe the toponym "Bohemia."

Starting from 35-34 BC, the Pannonians began to enter the sphere of influence of the Romans, who later made Pannonia a province, although a significant portion of the Pannonians nevertheless remained included in the nearby province of Noricum. Subjected to Latinization and, later, to Germanization, Slavicization, and Magyarization, the Pannonians—both of Celtic and Illyrian lineage—dissolved as an autonomous people from the first centuries of the first millennium.

9.   The Galates

The penetration of the Celts into the Balkan Peninsula is attested to by Greek sources, which testify to a migration that submerged Thrace in 281 BC. The Greeks, perhaps adapting a term employed by those same Celtic tribes, called the invaders γαλάται instead of κελτοί or κέλται—a term with which they identified the native inhabitants of the Greekized areas near the colony of Marseille.

Galatian incursions went as far as the heart of Greece. A horde, led by the leader Brenno, attacked Delphi, giving up only at the last minute to desecrate the temple of Apollo. Alarmed by portentous thunder and lightning, he also renounced to collect a ransom. Also in the third century BC, another fraction of the people, consisting of three tribes and ten thousand strong fighters accompanied by women, children, and slaves, moved from Thrace to Anatolia at the express invitation of Nicomedes I of Bithynia, who had asked for their help in the dynastic struggle that opposed him to his brother (278 BC).

The Galatians settled permanently in an area between eastern Phrygia and Cappadocia, in central Anatolia; following their settlement, the region took the name of "Galatia." San Girolamo attests to the survival of their language (Galato, a variety of continental Celtic) until the fourth century AD, after which the Hellenization process of the Galatians was completed.

10.   Latinization and Germanization

Celtiberi and Gauls were entirely Latinized in the first centuries of the Common Era; the assimilation of the vanquished concerned both the linguistic side, to the point of leading to the disappearance of the continental Celtic languages, and the socio-cultural one, with the extension of Roman citizenship and integration into the imperial political structures. The same fate fell to the Galatians, even if, in their case, the assimilating agent was of Greek origin.

The Pannonians and the Britons, on the other hand, were only partially Latinized, and in the regions they inhabited, Germanic elements took over—as early as the third century. If in Pannonia the assimilation of pre-existing populations was complete, also due to the successive Slavic and Magyar migratory waves, in the British Isles the process followed a different path.

Great Britain underwent, since the fourth century, a process of re-Celtization by groups from neighboring Ireland, which never entered the domains of Rome. Starting with St. Patrick's mission to Ireland (432), the island lost much of its Celtic heritage, dissolving ancient religions and myths. The first testimonies of the insular Celtic languages date back to these years—a resumption of the attestations of the Celtic languages after the oblivion that followed the extinction, at least in the testimonies, of the continental Celtic languages.

The expansion phase of the Irish Celts characterized the last centuries of the first millennium and affected mainly Scotland and the Isle of Man. This activity, however, was exclusively cultural and religious: From a political point of view, in fact, Ireland was invaded and controlled by the Germanic Vikings from the eighth to the ninth centuries, generating a Viking-Gaelic cultural syncretism.

11. The Society

Celtic society traced the fundamental structures of the Indo-European one, centered on the patriarchal "great family." This model was preserved by the Celts even in historical times; the family group (clan, a Scottish term that entered Italian) included not only the family in the strict sense but also ancestors, collaterals, descendants, and in-laws, including several dozen people. Several clans formed a tribe, at the head of which was a king. The family and not the individual also owned the land.

The social structure, known mainly thanks to the testimony given by Caesar about the Gauls in his Commentarii, was divided into classes. The warrior aristocracy performed the tasks of defense and offense and elected, according to a customary scheme among the Indo-Europeans, a king with mainly military functions, while the prerogative of the free people was economic activities, centered on agriculture and livestock. Then there is news of the existence of slaves. Finally, there were the druids, priests, magistrates, and magicians— custodians of community traditions, of collective knowledge, and of the intertribal identity in which all Celts recognized themselves. This identity was not limited to the single subgroups of the great Celtic family, but embraced it in its entirety; Caesar, in fact, repeatedly certifies the bonds that the Celtic Gauls were aware of having, not only among themselves but also with the nearby Helvetians, Belgians, Cisalpine Gauls, and Britons.

The woman enjoyed equal rights within Celtic society. She could inherit like men and be elected to any office, including that of druid or commander in chief of armies; this last possibility is attested to by the figures of Cartimandua of the Briganti tribe and Boudicca of the Iceni at the time of the Roman emperor Claudius.

12.   The Warriors and the Army

The armor of the Celts included wooden shields with bronze and iron finishes, with sculpted bronze animals. On their heads, they wore bronze helmets with large protruding figures like horns, forelegs of birds, or quadrupeds, which made those who wore them appear gigantic.

Their trumpets of war made a deafening and terrifying sound to the enemy. Some wore iron plates on their chests, while others fought naked. They used not only short swords similar to the Roman gladi but also long ones, anchored to iron or bronze chains, which hung along their right flank, as well as iron-tipped spears one cubit long and just under two wide. Their darts had points longer than the swords of other peoples.

13.   Celtic Daggers

It is also said of them that they preferred to resolve battles with duels between leaders or among the most skilled warriors of each of the opposing sides, rather than clash in battle. They had the habit of hanging the heads of slain enemies around the neck of their horses, and, in some cases, of embalming them, when the vanquished was an important opposing warrior; in fact, they considered the head, and not the heart, the seat of the soul.

The warrior vocation of these people, together with the prospect of obtaining a regular penny or occasional loot, eventually resulted in an activity practiced by many of their tribes: becoming mercenary soldiers. The first indication of such a choice dates back to 480 BC, when it seems that some Celtic soldiers participated, alongside the Carthaginians, in the battle of Imera. Other Celtic mercenary holdings are mentioned during the Syracusan expedition to Greece in 369-368 BC; in 307 BC, when three thousand armed Gauls joined Agatocle of Syracuse, together with Samnites and Etruscans, to lead a campaign in northern Africa; and in the struggles that followed between the heirs of Alexander the Great (the Diadochi). This practice not only generated an expanding market for several tens of thousands of courageous, experienced, and less expensive soldiers than the Greeks but also allowed, on the return of soldiers from wars fought almost everywhere in the Mediterranean basin, the introduction of coinage to the interior of Celtic communities.

14. Nature and Physical Appearance

The Celts were described by their Greek and Roman contemporaries as tall, muscular, and robust; the eyes were generally light, the skin clear, the hair frequently blond (also due to the custom described by Diodorus Siculus of lightening his hair with chalk water). The average height among men was around one meter and seventy. From the character point of view, the same sources describe the Celts as short-tempered, quarrelsome, valiant, loyal, heavy drinkers, and music lovers.

15. Religion

Cernunnos, the "horned god" of the Celts

The main testimony of Celtic beliefs and religious customs is once again that provided by Caesar in the De bello Gallico, which, although referring specifically to the Gauls, probably attests to a situation largely common to the entire Celtic group at the time of the facts narrated (first century BC).

The Celts probably shared the same polytheistic religious vision and worshiped divinities linked to nature, the oak, and the warrior virtues. Caesar also refers to the belief in the transmigration of souls, which resulted in an attenuation of the fear of death such as to strengthen the Gallic military value. It is also known, always among the Gauls, that human sacrifices were practiced; the victims offered themselves voluntarily. Alternatively, criminals were used, but innocent people were also sacrificed in case of need.

In the Gallic pantheon, Caesar testifies to the particular cult attributed to a god that he assimilates to the Roman Mercury, perhaps the Celtic god Lúg. He was the inventor of the arts, the travel guide, and the divinity of trade. Other prominent figures among the Gallic gods were "Apollo" (Belanu, the healer), "Mars" (Toutatis, the warlord), "Jupiter" (Taranis, the thunder lord), and "Minerva" (Belisama, initiator of the arts).

16. Celtic Laws

There is very little evidence of Celtic law. Caesar testifies, speaking of the Gauls, of a matrimonial law which provided for the joint administration between the spouses of the family patrimony, constituted in equal parts at the time of the wedding. Justice was administered by the druids, who had full discretion over the secrecy of the sentences.

17. Economy

The Celts routinely hunted and pillaged the cities and populations on which their raids fell; this habit is attested to in the entire area occupied by the Celts in antiquity, as evidenced, for example, by the Gallic incursions into Italy (sack of Rome, 390 BC) and Galatian raids in Greece (sack of Delphi, 279 BC).

In the places where the Celtic settlement was more extensive and lasting (Gauls and the British Isles), flourishing agriculture developed, which accompanied breeding, and metallurgical craftsmanship, with a peculiar and refined goldsmith's art, of which they constitute a characteristic element of torque, rigid necklaces in bronze, silver, or gold. From these regions, the Celts developed an extensive commercial network; in particular, tin from Britain was imported to the continent, where it was conveyed to the Mediterranean Sea. Here, in the cities of Narbonne Gaul (Marseille, Narbonne), commercial transactions took place with the Carthaginians, Greeks, and Etruscans and, later, the Romans.

18.   Agriculture

Skilled farmers, the Celts cultivated quadrangular fields, not very large; the average size was ten to fifteen ares, corresponding to what was possible to plow in a single day. The fields were bordered by hedges to protect them from the trampling of wild animals.

As early as the eighth century BC, the ability to work iron allowed the Celts to make axes, scythes, and other tools to clear out large-scale territories, previously occupied by impenetrable forests, and to work the land with ease. The growing skill in metalworking also allowed for the construction of new equipment, such as swords and spears, which made them militarily superior to their neighboring populations and enabled them to move with relative ease, as they did not fear other peoples. Extracted in a spongy form, the iron was subjected to a first forge processing and distributed in ingots, weighing five to six kilograms, with a bipyramidal shape. In a later period, the ingots were replaced by long flat bars, ready to be worked into long swords. Such bars were so popular that they were even used as money, along with copper and gold coins.

19.   Monetation

The use of the coin spread in the Celtic territories starting from the areas colonized by the Greeks, along the Mediterranean coast of Gaul. Since the third century BC, the Gauls used Greek coins, then passed later to Roman ones. The Celts also minted their own coins, both in Gaul and in the Iberian Peninsula (part of the so-called Hispanic coinage), inspired by the Greek and Roman ones.

Even among the Celts, the coin was a convenient means for quantifying a precious metal such as gold or silver, in transitions of a certain importance. Its introduction is to be found in the pay that was given as compensation to Celtic mercenaries (such as the Gesati). Therefore, the first appearances of local emissions in the Rhone river basin, following the return by the Jesuit mercenaries of the first half of the third century BC, would not be due to mere coincidence. The subsequent variations, in particular starting from the second century BC, were a means of marking the difference between the different territorial communities, with the progressive affirmation of the city-states. The obligation to distinguish each subsequent issue of the same oppidum, while maintaining its main and distinctive features, led engravers to develop a rare capacity for variation in the processing of ever more original images.

20.   Trade

In addition to the Mediterranean, the commercial relations of the Celts also developed toward the interior of the European continent; Celtic artifacts have been found in a large area of central Europe, at the time inhabited by Germans and other populations. For example, one of the finest examples of Celtic metallurgy, the Cauldron of Gundestrup (late second century BC), was found in Jutland.

The Celts were also responsible for the opening of most of the roads in northwestern Europe. The mere fact that Caesar, in his account of the conquest of Gaul, repeated several times that his troops moved so quickly through Gaulish territory, suggests how excellent the road system of this region was then. New confirmation of the excellence of Celtic road networks arrived in 1985, with the discovery, in the Irish county of Longford, of a stretch of road over nine hundred meters long, dating back to 150 BC. It had foundations of oak beams placed side by side, over bars of ash, oak, and alder. In the areas subjected to them, the Romans did nothing but replace the wood with stone, above the pre-existing paths built by the Celts.

21. Language

The main feature of the identification of Celtic peoples is their belonging to the same linguistic family, that of the Celtic languages. This family is part of the larger Indo-European group, from which it broke away in the third millennium BC. There are three main hypotheses that better specify the moment of separation of the common Celtic or proto-Celtic.

According to the first, the proto-Celtic would have developed in the area of La Tène culture starting from a wider "European whole." This linguistic continuum, extended in much of central-eastern Europe, was formed following a series of penetrations of Indo-European peoples in Europe, coming from their original Indo-European homeland (the steppes north of the Black Sea, cradle of the Kurgan culture). The detachment from the common trunk of this European ensemble is traced back to the first centuries of the third millennium BC, between approximately 2900 and 2700 BC.

The second hypothesis, which in any case starts from the same overall vision of the Indo-Europeanization of Europe, postulates a secondary penetration into central Europe (always in the area of La Tène, and always starting from the Kurganic steppes). This population movement, in this case exclusively Proto-Celtic, would be placed around 2400 BC. This postponement of the separation of Proto-Celtic from Indo-European is motivated by dialectological considerations, which underline some characteristics that Celtic languages share with later Indo-European languages including, in particular, Greek.

The third hypothesis moves from a radically different approach. It is the one, advanced by Colin Renfrew, which makes the Indo-Europeanization of Europe coincide with the spread of the Agricultural Revolution of the Neolithic (fifth millennium BC). The Proto-Celtic would, in this case, be the evolution that took place in situ, in the entire area historically occupied by the Celts (British

Isles, Iberian Peninsula, Gallie, Pannonia), of Indo-European. This hypothesis is supported in the archaeological field, but contested by linguists: The size of the area occupied by the Celts, the absence of political unity, and the long period of separation of the different varieties of Celtic (three thousand years from the common Celtic to the first historical attestations) are a set of factors considered incompatible with the close affinity between the various ancient Celtic languages, very similar to each other.

22.   The ancient Celtic languages

The Celtic languages attested to in antiquity, the first and direct result of the dialectal fragmentation of the common Celtic, are defined as continental Celtic languages due to the absence in this era of evidence of the varieties spoken by the Britons. Indirectly, however, it is possible to hypothesize that the differences between Gallic and British were not particularly profound: Caesar, in fact, testifies to close contacts—cultural, commercial, and political—between Gauls and Britons, describing them as extremely similar, even if not explicitly referring to their language. The ancient Celtic languages of which attestations are preserved (Gallic, Celtiberian, Lepontius, Galatian, and, to a very limited extent, Paleoironian) are testified to by a series of inscriptions and glosses in the Greek, Latin, and—limited to Celtiberian—Iberian alphabets, dated roughly between the fourth century BC and the fourth century AD.

The languages of the Celts in continental Europe all died out in the Imperial Roman age, under the pressure of Latin, the Germanic languages , and, in the case of Galato, Greek. The continental Celtic languages acted as a substrate in the formation of the new languages, Germanic or neo-Latin, which developed in the regions that hosted their speakers.

The Celts created their own heroic literature, of which, however, there is very little evidence. This literary tradition, in fact, was transmitted only orally, through the work of the bards and druids, according to what Caesar testified to the Gauls. The use of writing—in the Greek, Latin, or Iberian alphabet—was reserved for practical functions, as the transcription of wisdom (poetic and religious) was considered illicit among the Celts. Wishing to preserve its secrecy, the wise handed it down exclusively orally, dedicating many years of study and the use of mnemonics to this task. At a later age, however, part of the Celtic poetic corpus was still put in writing: The earliest evidence, in Irish, dates back to the sixth to seventh centuries.

Between the fourth and third centuries BC, the ornamental ironwork of the swords was very fine, incised, chiseled, die-forged. Cities, generally of modest size, were built on the tops of hills, which made them easy to defend.

The construction technique used by the Celts in the fortification of their citadels was that defined by the Romans murus gallicus. Caesar, in the De bello Gallico, describes it as a structure consisting of a wooden framework and stone fillings.

The goldsmith's art is the artistic branch of the ancient Celts of which the greatest testimonies have survived. Typical of Celtic craftsmanship, Gallic in particular, are the torques, necklaces, or bracelets made of gold, silver, or bronze. Other Celtic artifacts preserved are jewels, bowls, and cauldrons.

The metal objects, at the end of the processing, were embellished with applications of colored material. On numerous artifacts, in fact, starting from the fourth century BC, fusions of enamels, obtained with a particular red glass paste, were initially fixed using a fine iron mesh, together with the Mediterranean coral, directly on the objects, almost representing a magical form of blood, "petrified of the sea" and released from fire. Starting from the third century BC, polychrome glass bracelets were developed, with direct application and fusion of the enamel on swords and sets, without the use of support structures. New colors, such as yellow and blue, were introduced starting from the second to first centuries BC, although red remained the predominant color.

The Celts had a notable taste for bright colors, even on the fabrics that they used to make their clothes, as the modern Scottish tartans still testify to today. Diodorus Siculus says that "the Celts wore surprising clothes, dyed tunics in which all colors bloom, and trousers that they call 'breeches.' Above they wear short cloaks with multicolored stripes, tightened by fibulae, of furry fabric in winter and smooth summer."

Thus was born the Empire of the Gauls by the general Posthumus (260). However, he was soon killed by his own troops (268) and the secession of the Gallic provinces was repressed by Aureliano in 273. In the same period, the state of economic and social crisis pushed bands of bagaudi in revolt against the imperial authority to take refuge in wooded or less populated regions.

The Roman Empire managed to overcome the crisis and present itself with greater force under Diocletian (284 - 313 or 316) thanks to the institution of the Tetrarchy. The resistance of the Gallic bagaudi was weakened by Maximian, general of Diocletian and future emperor.

23.   Vandals 457-461

On the night of December 31, 406, the Roman Empire suffered a devastating invasion; favored by the cold that had closed the waters of the river in its grip, groups of Vandals, Suebi, Alani, and other Germanic peoples en masse crossed the imperial limes spanning the frozen Rhine. Despite the efforts and good military results of Flavius Ezio against the invaders, the imperial power in Gaul continued to lose ground and the cadres of the Empire disintegrated until the transfer of political power into the hands of the "kings"; this process continued until the fall of the Western Roman Empire in 476 AD.

Chapter 2: Welsh Mythology

Welsh mythology is the mythology of the people of the principality of Wales which is part of the mythology of the Brythonic people. These were the ancient Britons who inhabited the British Isles, including Cornwall, Ireland and Brittany the Isle of Man, and the Scottish Isles before the Roman invasion. Today Wales is a part of the United Kingdom and occupies the western part of the island of Great Britain between England in the east, the Bristol Channel in the south and the Irish Sea in the west and north.

The earliest Britons

According to recent research that has produced the first genetic map of the British Isles, the Welsh were found to be able to trace their DNA back to the period following the last Ice Age.

This is believed to make them the descendants of early pioneers who first settled Britain about 10,000 years ago.

Because of its mountainous terrain and westerly location Roman, Anglo-Saxon and Viking invaders never conquered or rarely mixed with the Welsh so there was not a similar spread of foreign genes as was experienced by other parts of Britain. Furthermore the research showed there was not a "Celtic" genetic group though the Welsh, Cornish, Northern Irish, and Scottish had the most differences from the rest of the UK.

The Welsh people as descendants of the original inhabitants of the British Isles before the Roman Conquest, still proudly retain their own unique language, culture, history, mythology and tradition that evolved from the ancient Britons and Celtic people before Christianity and developed through the ages. It later became influenced by Christianity and mixed with Medieval romance and culture to give the rich plethora of folklore, mythology and legend that we know today.

Surviving ancient books

Much of the early pre-Christian mythology and legends can still be seen in the surviving medieval literature of Wales, such as the Book of Taliesin, and the Book of Aneirin and the Mabinogion of the Red Book of Hergest, the White Book of Rhydderch. Other sources of Welsh mythology and legend are poems such as Cad Goddeu (The Battle of the Trees) and texts such as Thirteen Treasures of the Island of Britain the Welsh Triads which also contain much folklore and references to Arthurian legend and post-Roman Britain. Much of the early mythology before the Romans was not written down but learned and repeated orally by Celtic Druids so there is much that is unclear and many gaps to fill.

The Latin Historia Britonum (the History of the Britons) attributed to Nennius in the 9th century and Historia Regum Britanniae (the History of the Kings of Britain) by Geoffrey of Monmouth in the 12th century along with later works of folklore such as The Welsh Fairy Book by W. Jenkyn Thomas (1908) are also important reference points.

Myths, legends and folklore

Wales is rich in legend and culture has produced some marvelous stories. Below is just a small sample of the folktales and legends that seem to be found on every mountain, in every valley, every river bend, in the towns and villages of the Welsh people. In fact just about everywhere has some legend or tradition that takes you deep into the Welsh otherworld, and below are just a few.

•   King March's ears: The legend of King March's ears tells how a Welsh ruler born with unnaturally long ears tried to cover up his deformity. Eventually by supernatural means the truth came out. Despite his initial shame and anger he discovered that his appearance did not really matter to his subjects who loved him because of his kindness and because of the justness of his rule.

•   The Afanc of the River Conwy: The afanc was a type of supernatural water monster that lived in the rivers and lakes of ancient Wales. When angered they could make the waters rise to flood the land.

They would also kill and eat humans and animals. Hu Gadarn used his oxen to drag one to a pool on Snowdon where it could do no harm after it kept flooding the valleys.

•	The Lady of Llyn y Fan Fach: From Myddfai in Carmarthenshire comes the legend of the Lady of Llyn y Fan Fach, which tells how a local man fell in love and married a woman from the otherworld. Even though they enjoyed an idyllic relationship unfortunately it did not last and she was compelled to return to the Otherworld much to her husband's despair. She was the mother of three sons who became famous as the Physicians of Myddfai.

•	The Physicians of Myddfai: The three sons of the Lady of Llyn y Fan Fach practiced the skills of herbalism and healing that their mother had taught them. She taught them these special skills from the otherworld that they may alleviate pain and sickness in the world of humans and pass on that knowledge to others. They achieved renown with their skills and became known as the Physicians of Myddfai.

• Mereid of Cantre'r Gwaelod: Welsh legend and tradition tells how the sea drowned the land of Cantre'r Gwaelod which was also known as the Lost Hundred. There are a different versions but the story tells how a land of numerous villages was overwhelmed by the sea because of the human fallibility of Mereid the King's daughter who failed in her responsibility in taking care of a sacred well that dispersed the spirit of a goddess across the land.

• The birth of Taliesin: The tale of the legendary Taliesin tells of the most famous bards of the Welsh people. From his extraordinary birth to his life as a bard Taliesin holds a special place in Welsh legend, mythology and folklore.

• Hu Gadarn: Hugh Gadarn was a legendary leader and benefactor of the Welsh people. According to legend he led them from their original home of the Summer Country or Deffrobani to settle Britain. He was credited with giving them laws, teaching them how to pass on information in verse and how to plough the land. He also disposed of a water monster called the afanc which was causing floods across the land.

• Twm Siôn Cati: There are many legends in Wales that tell of the exploits of the legendary Twm Siôn Cati. He was born in the region of Tregaron and was a thief, outlaw and trickster for many years but did eventually settle to lead a more respectable life as a bard, historian and justice of the peace.

• Poetry and songs: These are just a few of the centuries old folktales and legends that abound in Wales. A great deal more of the folklore and traditions of Wales are found in poetry and songs that have been composed over the centuries. The Welsh language adds to the richness and depth to what amounts to a continuous growing bank of culture and tradition.

• The nature of myth: As is the nature of mythology, legend and folklore there are many different versions of the same tale. In some examples presented in these pages we offer interpretations of meaning though we recognize that myths and legends can be interpreted in many different ways and meaning may change with time. Therefore we encourage the reader to form their own opinions using their own experience and knowledge of the times they find themselves living in.

15 Amazing Welsh myths and legends

Wales is the land of dragons, wizards, King Arthur and the Holy Grail but did you know that the Devil is too embarrassed to visit Ceredigion?

That there's a village named after the country's bravest dog? Or that the Holy Grail itself ended up in a mansion near Aberystwyth?

1. Devil's Bridge: According to legend the Devil himself visited Ceredigion in the 11th century after hearing about its breathtaking scenery. While there, he struck a bargain with a local woman whose cow was stranded across the river. In a bid to buy her soul, the devil said he'd build her a bridge in exchange for the soul of the first living thing that crossed it.

When the bridge was built the woman threw a loaf of bread across it which her dog then chased.

The Devil was never seen in Wales again, too embarrassed at being outwitted by the old lady.

In the village of Devil's Bridge today there are three crossings across the river. The oldest is said to have been built by Satan himself.

2. The Lady of the Lake: The story goes that it was at Llyn y Fan Fach, a remote lake in the Black Mountains, where a young farmer named Gwyn won and then tragically lost the love of his life.

He fell in love with a beautiful woman who emerged from the water and she agreed to marry him but warned him she would leave him forever if he struck her three times.

They lived happily for many years and had three sons but when Gwyn struck her playfully for the third time she disappeared into the lake and he never saw her again.

She would sometimes re-appear to her sons and teach them the powers of healing with herbs and plants. They became skilful physicians, as did their children after them.

Some of their ancient remedies have survived and are in the Red Book of Hergest, one of Wales' most important medieval manuscripts.

3. Nanteos Cup: The cup is said to be the Holy Grail, used by Joseph of Arimathea to catch Christ's blood while interring Him in his tomb.

Medieval chroniclers claimed Joseph took the cup to Britain and founded a line of guardians to keep it safe. It ended up in Nanteos Mansion near Aberystwyth, attracting visitors who drank from it, believing it had healing powers.

The cup still exists with bits nibbled off by the sick in the hope of a miracle cure.

Belief in the cup's holy powers have persisted despite a 2004 television documentary in which experts found it dated from the 14th Century, some 1,400 years after the Cruxifiction. In July 2014, a police operation was launched to find it after it was stolen.

4. Cadair Idris: One of Wales' most iconic peaks, standing in southern Snowdonia, its name directly translates as Idris' Chair in reference to the mythical giant who once used the mountain as his throne.

There are numerous stories and legends associated with the mountain and Idris.

A few of the nearby lakes - such as Tal-y-llyn - are reputed to be bottomless, and those who venture up the mountain at night should take heed before sleeping on its slopes.

It is said that those who sleep on the mountain will awaken either as a madman, a poet or, indeed, never wake again.

5. Angelystor: Folklore says villagers in Llangernyw, midway between Abergele and Llanrwst, learn their grim fate from a supernatural being under the boughs of a 3,000-year-old yew tree.

Each year on Halloween and July 31 the Angelystor is said to appear in the medieval church of Llangernyw in Conwy.

On those dates it solemnly announces, in Welsh, the names of those parish members who will die shortly after.

The churchyard contains the oldest living thing in Wales - a yew tree which botanists believe to be over 3,000 years old.

6. Cantre'r Gwaelod: The kingdom of Maes Gwyddno, more commonly known as Cantre'r Gwaelod, is said to lie under the Irish Sea in Cardigan Bay.

It was ruled by Gwyddno Garanhir (Longshanks), born circa 520AD.

The land was said to be extremely fertile but depended on a dyke to protect it from the sea. The dyke had sluice gates which were opened at low tide to drain the water from the land, and closed as the tide returned.

In around 600AD, a storm blew up from the south west, driving the spring tide against the sea walls. The appointed watchman, Seithennin, a heavy drinker and friend of the king, was at a party in the king's palace near Aberystwyth.

Some say he fell asleep due to too much wine, or that he was too busy having fun, to notice the storm and to shut the gates.

The water gates were left open, and the sea rushed in to flood the land of the Cantref, drowning more than 16 villages.

7. Merlin's Oak: Merlin's Oak stood in the centre of Carmarthen amid the legend that King Arthur's famous wizard had placed a protective curse on it.

In local tradition, the wizard said Carmarthen would "drown" if the oak was ever removed, and some even said a curious, pointed notch in the tree was the face of Merlin himself.

In fact, the tree was poisoned in the 1850s by a local who objected to people holding meetings beneath it, but its trunk was preserved within iron railings.

It was then removed from the town when someone set it on fire at the end of the 1970s.

Carmarthen then suffered its worst floods for many years.

Bardsey Island off the coast of the Llyn peninsula, meanwhile, is said to be the burial place of Merlin who lies in a glass coffin surrounded by the 13 treasures of Britain and nine bardic companions.

8. Gelert: The village of Beddgelert in Gwynedd literally means Gelert's Grave and is supposedly the final resting place of Wales' most famous dog.

The canine belonged to Llywelyn the Great, Prince of Gwynedd, who one day was out hunting with his wife, leaving their baby son with a nurse and a servant to look after him.

The nurse and the servant went for a walk in the mountains leaving the baby alone. When Llewelyn returned Gelert came running out of the lodge towards his master, covered in blood.

Llewelyn rushed into the baby's room to find the cradle overturned and no sign of his son.

Filled with grief he drew his sword and killed Gelert. As the dog died his whimpers were answered by the sound of a baby crying from behind the overturned cradle.

When Llewelyn pulled aside the cradle he found his son unharmed and the body of a huge wolf next to him.

With huge remorse, Llewelyn buried Gelert in a meadow nearby and marked his grave with a cairn of stones.

9. Twm Sion Cati: Dubbed the Welsh Robin Hood, Twm Sion Cati was actually a bard and genealogist called Thomas Jones who lived in Tregaron from 1530 to 1620.

He became a highwayman robbing the rich but it appears he was a bit tight-fisted and didn't distribute a penny to the poor.

He was reputed to be a trickster and a master of deception. But he also had a soft side – he avoided maiming his victims and preferred to pin them with a well-aimed arrow to their saddles.

He hid from the Sheriff of Carmarthen in the wooded slopes of Dinas Hill, close to

Rhandirmwyn, and his cave today is well hidden on the banks of the river Towy in the RSPB sanctuary of Dinas Hill.

10. King Arthur: Arthur is heavily associated with Wales. The lakes of Llydaw, Dinas and Ogwen, are amongst those that claim to contain the magical Excalibur.

A stone reputedly bearing the hoof print of Arthur's horse Llamrai can be found on the banks of Lake Barfog near Betws y Coed.

It is said that the mark was made when Arthur and his horse dragged a monster from the lake's deep waters.

Arthur is also associated with Mount Snowdon, where he reputedly killed the mountain's most famous resident - Rhitta, a fearsome giant who created a cape for himself out of the beards of his enemies. His corpse was covered in huge stones by Arthur's men at the summit of the mountain.

11. Dinas Emrys: Located near Beddgelert is Dinas Emrys, the lofty mountain home of the Welsh red dragon.

In the fifth century the Celtic King Vortigern chose the area as the site for his castle.

Every day his men would work hard erecting the first of several proposed towers; but the next morning they would return to find the masonry collapsed in a heap.

Vortigern was advised to seek the help of a young boy who turned out to be Merlin.

He explained that the hill fort could not stand due to a hidden pool containing two dragons. Vortigern commanded his labourers to dig deep into the mountain and they did indeed discover an underground lake.

Once drained, the red and white dragons that lay sleeping there awoke and began to fight.

The white dragon represented the Saxons and the red dragon the Welsh. Eventually the white dragon fled and the red dragon returned quietly to his lair.

Vortigern's castle was built and duly named after Dinas Emrys. The red dragon has been celebrated ever since.

12. The Afanc: A lake monster from Welsh mythology, the afanc can also be traced through references in British and Celtic folklore.

Sometimes described as taking the form of a crocodile, giant beaver or dwarf, it is also said to be a demonic creature.

The afanc was said to attack and devour anyone who entered its waters.

Various versions of the tale are known to have existed. In one telling the wild thrashings of the afanc caused flooding which drowned all the people of Britain.

Several sites lay claim to its domain, among them Llyn Llion, Llyn Barfog and Llyn-yr-Afanc (the Afanc Pool), a lake in Betws-y-Coed.

13. Madoc: Prince Madoc was the son of Owain Gwynedd, one of the greatest and most important rulers in the country.

In 1170 Owain died and, almost immediately, a violent and very bloody dispute arose between his 13 children regarding the succession.

Madoc and his brother Rhirid were so upset and angered by events that they decided they wanted nothing more to do with their family or their homeland.

They duly took ship from Rhos on Sea and sailed westwards to see what they could find.

What Prince Madoc found, so the legend runs, was America. He and his brother managed to cross the Atlantic and land on the shores of the New World.

His sailors inter-married with a local Native American tribe, and for years the rumour of Welsh-speaking Native American tribes was widely believed.

14. St David: Born around the year 520 on the cliffs in a wild thunderstorm near the city that's now named after him, David was believed to be the son of Sanctus, king of Ceredigion and a nun called Nonnita (Non).

Stories of St David's miracles include bringing a dead boy back to life by splashing the child's face with tears and restoring a blind man's sight.

David's best-known miracle allegedly took place in the village of Llanddewi Brefi.

He was preaching to a large crowd, but some people had difficulty hearing him.

Suddenly a white dove landed on David's shoulder, and as it did, the ground on which he stood rose up to form a hill, making it possible for everyone to see and hear him. Today, a church stands on the top of this hill.

15. Mabinogion: The Mabinogion is a collection of tales taken from medieval Welsh manuscripts. Based partly on historical events, many recount myths and legends dating from the 11th century.

The complex stories are set in a bizarre and magical landscape which corresponds geographically to the western coast of Wales and are full of white horses that appear magically, giants, beautiful, intelligent women and heroic men.

IRISH MYTHOLOGY

Like most things Irish, it all started with the Celts. This band of tribes, warriors and farmers originated in the central European Alps, and spread out to occupy almost the entire European continent long before the ancient Romans became such a dominant force. At the peak of their power, they had inhabited everywhere between what is now Ireland in the west and Turkey in the east. Around 225 BC, the Celts suffered their first major defeat at the hands of the Romans, and over the next few centuries more attacks came. Since they had no form of centralised government or organisation (they were each separate tribes who operated independently, only bound by language, customs and religion), they gradually declined. Except, that is, for the areas where the Romans and other societies never managed to reach; namely Ireland, Scotland, the Isle of Man, Wales, Cornwall in England and Brittany in France.

Celtic society was rich and complex. They placed great emphasis on war and victory, and viewed nobility, religion, wealth and beauty as hugely important. They were skilled craftsmen and created exquisite jewellery and decorative objects from gold, copper and bronze. They had an astronomical calendar and celebrated various festivals in honour of their gods and goddesses, constructing impressive monuments and tombs to honour their dead that were aligned with the stars. Nature was also important to them, with trees, animals and the natural elements considered sacred. However, despite all of this obvious intelligence, there is no evidence of them using any form of writing apart from a primitive line script known as Ogham. They were almost entirely an oral society, passing their knowledge and skills through the generations through word of mouth and demonstration.

For that very reason, it is only through other sources that we have come to know the mythology of the Celts. The first mentions come from Roman sources, although since the Celts and the Romans were mortal enemies, anything written down by them was done so with an air of derision rather than an attempt at recording or understanding the complex stories. It was only when the first Christian missionaries came to Ireland and began converting the remaining Celts that some forward thinking monks began collecting the stories and writing them down, both for posterity's sake and most likely to use as a tool for understanding the society in order to win them over to the Christian way of life. As the stories passed down from generation to generation and then later to the monks, elements of them were lost, added to, misunderstood, and so on, further developing the stories into the vast lexicon we have now gathered today.

What is Irish Mythology?

Irish mythology refers to the traditional pre-Christian stories told by the Irish, or Gaelic, people and other closely related groups. Many of these stories take show how Ireland came to be settled by the Gaels, how specific natural features of Ireland came to be, or record the adventures of mythic heroes who may or may not have a basis in fact.

When Ireland became Christianized by St. Patrick and his followers, the Irish people recorded these stories in writing and preserved them for centuries. In doing so, they created some of the earliest vernacular literature in Europe. These stories were broken up into four distinct cycles, or groups of tales:

• the Mythological Cycle, which covers the settling of Ireland by the Gods and the arrival of the Irish people.

• the Cycle of Kings, which cover stories of the early Irish kings, warriors and heroes.

• the Ulster Cycle, which take place during the golden age of Ulster under the reign of Conchobar mac Nessa.

• the Fenian Cycle, which focus on a band of warriors known as the Fenians who guard Ireland from foreign invaders.

Two of them, the Ulster and Fenian Cycles focus on the lives and adventures of two of the greatest heroes of Irish mythology; Cuchullain and Finn McCool.

Cu Chulainn

Cu Chulainn was a mythical Irish warrior and champion of Ulster, also referred to as Cuchulainn, Cuchullain and Setanta

The great Irish hero Cu Chulainn is to Irish Mythology, what Achilles is to Greek Mythology. Both brave warriors were undefeatable in battle and both were demigods. Cu Chulainn was the most prominent of Hero of Ulster and his story is told largely in within the Ulster Cycle of Irish Mythology.

The legend of Cu Chulainn tells how he was the son of the God Lugh and was born at Newgrange, Ireland's most prominent Neolithic monument. The most famous of Cu Chulainn's legends is the Cattle Raid of Cooley as told in the Tain. In this tale Cu Chulainn, single-handed fought the armies of Queen Mebh of Connacht. After the army of Ulster had been put to sleep by Queen Mebh's magic, Cu Chulainn was left to defend Ulster's lands taking on champions after champion one in single combat that lasted months.

Cu Chulainn was eventually killed after Queen Mebh contrived with his enemies to bring him to battle. She put a spell on the mighty warrior and he became mortally wounded by the spear of Lugaid. But Cuchulainn fought on causing his enemies to retreat. Cu Chulainn then tied himself to a rock to keep himself standing so that his enemies wouldn't think he was wounded. The ploy almost worked, when a raven landed on his shoulder. Cu Chulainn's enemies returned to finish him off but not before Cu Chulainn was able to deliver a fatal blow to Lugaid.

Today Cu Chulainn is still hailed as one of Ireland's great heroes. In Ulster he is hailed as a hero by both Irish Nationalists and Ulster Unionists and is regularly depicted in poetry, literature and other art forms in Ireland.

Fionn Mac Cumhail

Fionn Mac Cumhail or Finn MacCool was the legendary Irish warrior/hunter who led the band of Irish warriors known as the Fianna and created the Giants Causeway.

Fionn is connected to many of the legends of the Fenian Cycle. He first came to prominence after catching and eating the Salmon of Knowledge. Another important legend tells how Fionn met his first wife Sadbh while hunting. She had been transformed into a deer by a druid and after Fionn, caught her she turned into a beautiful woman. She bore Fionn a child, Oisin, before befing transformed again into a deer and separating Fionn from his son for many years. Another tale tells of how Fionn in a jealous rage, pursued the lovers Grainne and Diarmuid across Ireland after they had eloped together.But the most famous legend of Fionn Mac Cumhail surrounds the Giants Causeway in Country Antrim.

The story goes that Fionn built the causeway to get to Scotland and battle with a rival giant called Benandonner. When he got there he found that the Scottish giant was asleep but also far bigger than himself, so Fionn returned back across the causeway. When Benandonner woke up he came across the causeway intent on fighting Fionn. Fionn's wife dressed up her husband as a baby and when Benandonner arrived she said Fionn wasn't home and to be quiet not to wake up the baby. When Benandonner saw the baby he decided that if the baby was that big, Fionn must be massive. So he turned tail and fled back across the causeway ripping it up as he went. All that remains are the ends, here at the Giant's Causeway and on the island of Staffa in Scotland where similar formations are found.

Cycles of Irish mythology

Irish mythology can be divided into four main cycles, in chronological order. Within each cycle there are many different stories and characters, some important and some not so important, but all regularly occurring. In many cases the stories also interweave with one another, making it even more confusing! The four main cycles are:

Mythological Cycle

The Mythological cycle is the earliest one, and recounts the tales of the Tuatha de Danann or 'people of Danann', who were the mythological descendants of the Goddess Danann, the ancestors of the Irish Celts, and the first people to inhabit the island (allegedly). The Tuatha de Danann were demigods, stunningly beautiful and expertly skilled in music and the arts, with magical powers to boot. The mythological cycle is largely concerned with how Ireland first came to be inhabited and the various struggles for ownership that ensued. The Tuatha de Danann were led to Ireland by a woman named Cesair. Soon after they arrived a great flood wipes them all out except for one lucky survivor, Fintan. Fintan oversees the later settlements in animal form, the first unsuccessful one led by Partholan, and the second led by Nemed. Nemed's settlement breaks up into three groups, one of which leaves Ireland. The other two, the original Tuatha De Danann and the Fir Bolg, spend many years fighting before eventually learning to live in peace.

The drama doesn't stop there, however. Another band of warriors, the Fomoire, turn up to cause trouble, leading to two Gods arising from the Tuatha de Danann. One is Lug, master of the arts and warfare; the other is Dagda, the great God with a magical cauldron. The Fomoire and Tuatha have a huge battle known as the Second Battle of Mag Tuired. The Tuatha are victorius, but only until yet another tribe, the Sons of Mil, come along. The Sons of Mil are said to be the immediate ancestors of the Celts, and won the land by vanquishing the Tuatha to the underworld, where they now rule over the fairies.

Ulster Cycle

Up next is the Ulster cycle, the stories from which are much better known than the Mythological cycle. They focus on the warriors of King Conchabar, one of whom is known by everyone in Ireland: Cu Chulainn. Cu Chulainn is more or less the main character of the Ulster cycle, and all of the stories of his life are recounted. However, the Cu Chulainn in the mythological texts is not quite the same as the one from children's stories. While he is an athletic man and the ultimate warrior, he also has a number of more grotesque features when he heads into battle; he grows in size, one eye rolls back into his head, his hair stands on end with drops of blood on the end of each hair, and he attacks anyone in the vicinity regardless of whether they're a friend or an enemy! Some versions also claim he transforms completely into a non-human beast.

Another prominent character is Deirdre, whose tragic tale has inspired many modern Irish writers and creative types. She was unwillingly betrothed to King Conchobar, but instead fell in love with one of his warriors Naoise and escapes. When captured, she smashes her own head against a rock because she would rather die than be apart from her true love. The most famous story however is that of the Tain Bo Cuailgne, or Cattle Raid of Cooley, which features the ferocious Queen Medb. She raises an enormous army to raid the Cooley peninsula and steal the king's most prized bull for herself (in those days, wealth was measured in cattle). The Ulster cycle differs from the other cycles in that it is the only one that has no mention of a centralised hierarchy of kings or government, and involves many unrelated stories of warring small tribes and regions.

Fenian Cycle

The Fenian cycle is the third cycle of Irish mythology, and is largely focused on the legendary warrior Fionn MacCumhaill and his band of loyal followers, the Fianna. While the Mythological cycle is based on the ancient gods and the Ulster cycle on the various conflicts between different regions, the Fenian cycle is all about the cult and institution of warriors. It starts off with the origins of the Fianna, formed by the High King Cormac MacAirt with warriors from each clan in order to protect his kingdom. One of the most significant leaders of the Fianna, Cumhal, is brutally killed, and his wife flees to a safe place in order to give birth to his son in secret (she feared he would be chased down and murdered too if anyone knew of his existence). The son was Denma, later nicknamed Fionn because of his bright blonde hair.

The rest of the cycle charts the various events of Fionn's life, including his avenging of his father's death, his time studying with the poet Fin Eces. There he accidentally eats the magical salmon of knowledge and gains all the wisdom of the world, and is admitted to the court of the High King of Tara after rigorous tests. He Quickly impresses everyone and is made leader of the Fianna after he saved everyone from a malicious goblin who had been terrorising them at a big feast every year. He also met his wife, who had been trapped inside a deer's body by an evil druid, until she turned back into a fawn again after giving birth to their son, Oisin. From there, the cycle gets more and more interwoven with other stories, and becomes much too complicated for a simple summary! After a series of events, a huge battle at Gabhra culminates in the death of Fionn and the majority of his followers. Fionn's son Oisin is among the survivors.

Historical Cycle

The final cycle of Irish mythology is the Historical cycle, which deals with the institution and founding of great and lesser kings of Ireland. This cycle was written by the bards of the king's courts and blends mythology with historical detail. The main characters range from the almost entirely mythological Labraid Loingsech to the entirely historical Brian Boru, and include many other familiar characters. This cycle dates from after the coming of Christianity and Saint Patrick, and so has been influenced much more by Christian teachings than the other cycles.

Some of the most significant characters in the Historical cycle include; Cormac Mac Airt, founder of the Fianna, who's dramatic life takes up a large portion of the cycle; King Conn of the Hundred Battles, founder of Connacht who was famous for his fighting prowess and for making the coronation stone of Tara roar when he stepped on it (meaning that he was Ireland's rightful ruler); and Niall of the Nine Hostages who was the ancestor of the powerful O'Neill clan. His nickname comes from a particularly tense battle when he took 9 hostages, one from each province of Ireland as well as one from the Scots, Saxons, Britons and Franks. His legacy has endured right up until today; O'Neill is still in the top 10 most common surnames of Ireland.

Chapter 3: The Dagda

The Dagda is chief of the Tuatha dé Danann, the foremost of the Irish ancestral gods. Highly skilled and wise beyond measure, he is god of life and death, of seasons and agriculture and fertility, and of magic and druidry. He wields three sacred treasures: a cauldron of plenty, a club of life and death, and a harp that controlled men and the seasons alike.

His children are plentiful, as are his lovers. His dwelling place is Brú na Bóinne.

Etymology

The Dagda (Gaelic: An Dagda) is a title, meaning "the good or great god," reflecting his mastery of many skills rather than his character. This Gaelic name is derived from the Proto-Indo-European Dhagho-deiwos, or "shining divinity," and the later Proto-Celtic Dago-deiwos, where Dagos has two meanings: "shining" in relation to day time, or "good" as in skilled.

Beyond the Dagda, his many titles include Eochaid Ollathair (Horseman or All-Father), Fer Benn (the Horned Man), Ruad Rofhessa (Lord of Great Knowledge), Dáire (the Fertile One), and Cerrce (Striker), among others.

Attributes

As the "great god," the Dagda's skills gave him dominion over a wide range. He is the god of life and death, and of fertility and agriculture. He could set the seasons to order with a strum of his harp; he could slay or resurrect a man with his club; he was a generous lord of plenty. He is a druid, and has mastery over all things mystic and magic.

The Dagda is described as a giant of a man, oafish in demeanor and attire. His beard is long and unruly, and he wears a woolen cloak about his head. These clothes never fit right, exposing his stomach and buttocks. These faults did little to distract from his good looks. Some scholars theorize that this gruffness may come from the Christian recorders of Irish traditions, wishing to make the Dagda comedic and foolish. Even then, the Dagda is portrayed consistently as wise, witty, and wily, a druid schooled in magic, art, and military strategy.

The Dagda carried with him three sacred relics which defined his many talents.

In additions to these, the Dagda also has two pigs, one always growing, the other roasting, and an orchard ever bearing sweet fruit.

The Dagda's primary dwelling was at Brú na Bóinne, a series of Neolithic mounds on the banks of the River Boyne in County Meath. Historically, these mounds were constructed near 3200 BCE, older than Stonehenge or the Great Pyramids. One mound, called Newgrange, lines up with the dawn of the winter solstice, paralleling the Dagda's significance as the lord of seasons and his mastery the day and night.

Family Tree

As chief of the Tuatha dé Danann, the Dagda has many children, chief among them being Aengus, Brigid, and Midir. His lovers are plentiful, but the most notable are his spouse, the fearful Morrigan, and the river goddess Boann.

The Dagda's parentage varies. His parents are sometimes Elatha and Ethniu, who in some tales is the daughter of King Balor, while in others his father is Badurn. His brothers are often listed as Nuada, king of the gods, and Oghma, a great champion. They may be a triple god, sharing similar attributes as well as all three carrying contradictory titles such as chief or king at the same time. In many myths they coexist in a kind of hierarchy, with Nuada as king, the Dagda as chief and advisor, and Oghma as their champion.

Mythology

In addition to his mighty club, the Dagda also possessed a large cauldron. The cauldron was magical in that it had an endless supply of food in it—the ladle itself was said to be so large that two men could lie in it. The Dagda is typically portrayed as a plump man with a large phallus, representative of his status as a god of abundance. Some scholars believe that the Dagda's permanently erect phallus—so big it often dragged the ground was added later by Christian chroniclers who wished to turn him into a comical figure.

The Dagda held a position as a god of knowledge as well. He was revered by many Druid priests, because he bestowed wisdom upon those who wished to learn. He had an affair with the wife of Nechtan, a minor Irish god. When his lover, Boann, became pregnant Dagda made the sun stop setting for nine entire months. In this way, their son Aonghus was conceived and born in just one day.

When the Tuatha were forced into hiding during the invasions of Ireland, the Dagda chose to divide their land among the gods. Dagda refused to give a section to his son, Aonghus, because he wanted Aonghus' lands for himself. When Aonghus saw what his father had done, he tricked the Dagda into surrendering the land, leaving Dagda with no land or power at all.

•   Origins: The Lebor Gabála Érenn lays out the coming of the Tuatha dé Danann, the fifth group of settlers of mythical Ireland. They came from north of the Emerald Isle, hailing from four cities where they learned the sciences and arts of their time, including magic. At this time, the Dagda was chief, though not king. The Dagda was consulted and respected by all, even above their kings.

•   The courting of boann: The Dagda fell for Boann, goddess of the River Boyne and wife of Elcmar, a judge of the Tuatha dé Danann. To carry on this affair, he sent Elcmar to High King Bres, and soon Boann fell pregnant. To prevent retribution against the child, the Dagda held the sun in place for nine months, allowing Boann to carry and give birth to the child in a single day. This child was given by the Dagda to his son Midir to raise, and became, Aengus, god of love and poetry.

•   Brú Na Bóinne: In time Aengus grew to manhood, and the Dagda helped him trick Elcmar out of his rightful home at Brú na Bóinne. Using a carefully worded ploy befitting the gods of wisdom and poetry, they asked Elcmar to allow them to dwell there for "a day and a night." This phrasing in Old Irish has two meanings: a literal day and a night, and all days and nights, or eternity. In agreeing to this, Elcmar unwittingly gave his home to his enemies for eternity. Soon after, the Dagda and Boann assisted Aengus in his quest to search for the girl haunting his dreams.

Another myth tells that while Aengus was away, the Dagda gave out his land among his many children. Upon his return Aengus discovered his father had saved nothing for him, and using the same careful wording by which they had gained their home, the Dagda also unwittingly gave Brú na Bóinne to his son.

• The Second Battle Of Moytura: Upon arrival in Ireland the Tuatha dé Danann consolidated power by eliminating or conquering earlier settlers. The most powerful of these was the Fomorians, a monstrous race ruled by a cruel king named Balor. Knowing conflict was inevitable, the Dagda made careful plans, tricking the

Fomorians out of key resources, chief among them being sheep. On Samhain, the end of the Celtic year, he went to his wife, the Morrigan, goddess of battle and of death, and found her bathing. After they made love, she prophesied the coming battle: they would be victorious over the Formorions, at a price.

• At last, both sides met at Moytura, located in County Sligo, where they fought for control of Ireland. The fighting was fierce, laying low both Balor and the Dagda's brother Nuada. The Dagda himself was mortally wounded by Cethlenn, wife of Balor and herself a wise woman. During the battle, his magic harp was stolen, though it was ultimately recovered. Nursing his wound, the Dagda returned to Brú na Bóinne, where he succumbed and laid to rest in the mounds. He had ruled for seventy or eighty years, depending on source.

Like many of the Tuatha dé Danann, he may still be consulted by those visiting the fairymounds, and those who drift dangerously into the Otherworld.

• Outside Of Ireland: While not as explicit as Brigid or Lugh in the rest of the Celtic world, the Dagda is not without counterparts. Wise gods wielding powerful clubs and cauldrons of plenty are found in both France and Great Britain. The Gaullish Sucellus carries a hammer and a cup or barrel, and rules over agriculture. Dorset's Cerne Abbas Giant, a nameless giant wielding a club with an erection, may represent one of the Dagda's counterparts.

He is often compared to the Germanic Odin and the Roman Dis Pater, both gods carrying aspects similar to the Dagda.

Chapter 4: Lugh/Lug

For the Celts, who lived in central Europe, Lugh was a Sun god. The underworld god Balor was his grandfather. Balor was the leader of the Fomorii. The Fomorii were evil people that lived in the underworld.

According to a prophecy, Balor was to be killed by a grandson. To prevent the happening of the prophecy, Balor tried to kill his grandson, but Lugh miraculously survived. Lugh was secretly raised by the god of the sea ,Manannan, and became an expert warrior.

When he reached manhood, he joined the peoples of the goddess Dana, named the Tuatha De Danaan, to help them in their struggle against the Fomorii and Balor. Balor had an evil eye capable of killing whomever looked at it. Lugh threw a magic stone ball into Balor's eye, and killed Balor.

Lugh corresponds to the Welsh god Lleu and the Gallic Lugos. From Lugh's name derives the names of modern cities such as Lyon, Laon and Leyden. Today, people remember the figure of Lugh with a festival which commemorates the beginning of the harvest in August.

Who Is Lugh The Great Celtic God?

Lugh was born from the relationship of Ethne, the daughter of the Fomorian king Balor and a young man, Cian (Kian) who belonged to Tuatha Dé Danann and in our earlier article on Ancient Pages, we described how Lugh came into the world. Tailtiu was Lugh's foster-mother and his adoptive father was the god of the sea, Manannán mac Lir, who was older than the Tuatha de Danaan tribe people but considered as one of them.

Lugh, of the Long Arm, is the Irish god of nobility, a master of many crafts and a cunning warrior. He is both Ollamh Érenn and King of the Tuatha Dé Danann, and wields the Spear of Assal, which none can stand against.

His dwellings are at Tara in County Meath, and at Moytura in County Sligo. His holy day is Lughnasa, on August 1st.

Etymology

Lugh, sometimes spelled Lug, is a popular name in Ireland and throughout the Celtic world, but consensus on its meaning is debated. One suggestion is the Proto-Indo-European root lewgh-, meaning "to bind by oath," referencing his role over oaths and contracts. Others suggest a connection to light, but modern scholars find this unlikely.

His titles are numerous, but the most famous is Lámfada, "Of the Long Arm," a reference to the length of his spear in battle. Alternately it could be translated to "Artful Hands," showing his skill in craftsmanship. He is Ildánach (the Skilled God), mac Ethleen/Ethnenn (son of Ethliu/Ethniu, his Fomorian mother) and mac Cien (son of Cian, his Tuatha Dé Danann father); he is Macnia (the Youthful Warrior), Lonnbéimnech (the Fierce Striker), and Conmac (Son of the Hound).

Lugh was also the first to hold the title Ollamh Érenn, or Chief Ollam of Ireland. This historic title reflected his skills as a poet, a judge, and a ruler, and was a high position in each Irish court. While each kingdom had an ollam that served the chief or king, the High Kings of Ireland each had their own Chief Ollam.

Attributes

• Skills And Domains: Lugh is a master of many talents. He is the god of oaths, granting domain over rulers and nobility. He is also god of justice in its many forms, often without mercy. Despite these roles he was also a trickster, willing to lie, steal, and cheat to overcome his opponents.

His unique heritage, as son of the Tuatha Dé Danann and Fomorians, coupled with his fostering, put him in the position to invent a number of notable Irish games, including horse-racing, sports, and the Irish precursor to chess, fidchell.

• Sites: Several locations are named for him across Europe, but in Ireland specifically County Louth and the village of the same name bear his name, as does Loch Lugborta. Lugh had two dwellings: one at the place where he became king, Moytura in County Sligo, and a second at the dwelling at Tara, in County Meath. It is here that the historical High Kings of Ireland were seated.

• Holy Day: Lughasa (Lughnasadh), the Irish harvest festival, takes place on August 1st and is celebrated across Ireland, Scotland, and the Isle of Man. This date was chosen because it marked the victory of Lugh over the spirits of Tír na nÓg. On this day he blessed the early fruits of harvest, and held games and revelry, in memory of his foster-mother Tailtiu. It has various Christian names, including "Garland Sunday" or "Mountain Sunday," as many climb hills or mountains on this day. Lughnasa is also celebrated by many neo-pagan communities.

Family

Lugh is descended from two bloodlines: his father, Cian, is the son of Dian Cedh, healer of the Tuatha Dé Danann; his mother, Ethniu, is the daughter of King Balor of the dreaded Fomorians.

He was fostered, with different stories giving different parents: the Irish sea god, Manannán mac Lir; Tailtiu, Queen of the Firbolg; and Gavida, god of the smiths.

Lugh had many wives, including wives Buí, Buach, and Nás, the latter the daughter of a king of Britain who bore his son Ibic. By the mortal woman Deichtine he had his most famous son, Cúchulain, the great hero of the Ulster saga.

Mythology

Lugh is one of the most prominent figures in Irish cycles and folklore, in equal parts as savior and trickster.

• Origins: Numerous legends exist regarding the birth of Lugh. Cath Maig Tuired gives the marriage of Cian and Ethniu as a dynastic union between the invading Tuatha Dé Danann and the Formorians of Ireland. A later folktale differs: a prophecy warned that King Balor of the Fomorians would be slain by his grandson. Thus Balor hid his daughter Ethniu in a tower on Tory Island. Cian used the magic of a fairy woman named Biróg to transport himself there and seduced Ethniu, who gave birth to triplets. Balor forced a servant to drown them, and two died. One fell into the harbor and was rescued by Biróg, who took him to his father. Cian fostered Lugh to protect him.

• Joining The Tuatha: After coming of age, Lugh arrived at Tara, the hall of Nuada, king of the Tuatha Dé Danann. Court policy required any who entered to offer a skill to serve the king. Lugh offered many skills, but each time the doorkeeper stated that role was already filled. Thinking ⁇uickly, Lugh asked if the court had a master of every skill, to which the doorkeeper replied they did not. Thus he is allowed to join the court of Nuada as Chief Ollam, master of all skills.

In time, sensing that Lugh could bring salvation to the Tuatha Dé Danann, Nuada put Lugh in charge of the coming war against the Fomorians. Before that war could proceed, the First Battle of Moytura took place in County Galway against the Firbolg. There Nuada lost his hand, forcing him to step down as High King: a king cannot be blemished. His replacement was

Bres, a half-Fomorian who delayed war against his kin.

• The Sons Of Tuireann: Meanwhile, Cian met his end by the hand of Tuireann, his great foe. Tuireann's sons, Brian, Iuchar, and Iucharba, hunted down Cian, who had transformed into a pig. Before the final blow was struck, he transformed back into his human form, granting legal right to seek revenge to Cian's heir. The Sons of Tuireann attempted to bury Cian, but twice the ground spat him up. After the third burial, Lugh happened upon the grave and asked the ground who lay there, and it replied it was his father's grave. Lugh began to plot his revenge.

He invited the sons of Tuireann to a grand feast, and there asked them what they would require if their father was murdered. They replied that death was the only just response, and thus Lugh's trap was sprung: he revealed he was Cian's heir and thus demanded that same justice. As a god of games, he gave them a series of tasks, but they overcame each. Seeing the final task as impossible Tuireann pleaded for mercy for his sons but Lugh would not relent. The final task mortally wounded each, and Lugh withheld their magic pigskin that would have healed their wounds. Thus the Sons of Tuireann died, and in his grief, Tuireann too died, giving Lugh justice and victory over his father's enemies.

• Cath Maig Tuireg: For twenty-seven years King Bres forced the Tuatha Dé Danann to pay tribute to the Fomorians and work as slaves for their enemies. Lugh's grandfather and uncle crafted first a silver hand and then a hand of flesh for Nuada, thus removing his blemish: Nuada retook the throne and Bres was exiled. Lugh finished planning for war, seeking the counsel of the Phantom Queen, the Mórrígan. The Tuatha Dé Danann thus declared war.

The two armies met at Moytura in County Sligo, and Lugh fought fiercely with Assal and his sling. His grandfather Balor found Nuada in the fighting, and there beheaded him. But before Balor could claim victory, Lugh threw a stone with his sling at Balor's eye. Balor fell dead and the tide turned, the

Fomorians driven into the sea. Lugh was declared King of the Tuatha Dé Danann for his deeds. After the battle Bres, who fought for the Fomorians, was brought before him and begged for mercy. Lugh demanded Bres teach the Tuatha Dé Danann to plough the land in return, and Bres agreed.

Thus Lugh became King, and reigned over a united Ireland.

• Later Life And Death: The Tuatha Dé Danann never forgave Bres, and after learning to farm Lugh sought to finish him. He crafted three hundred wooden cows and filled them with poisoned red milk. Offering the milk to Bres, who could not deny such a hospitable offer, the former king drank each pail of milk without hesitation and died.

Lugh met his own end after his wife Buach took Cermait, son of the Dagda, as a lover. Upon discovering this Lugh killed him. In response, Cermait's three sons sought vengeance and drowned him in a lake, thus giving it the name Loch Lugborta. Lugh had ruled for forty years, and his end marked the decline of the Tuatha Dé Danann.

After his death, Lugh dwelled in Tír na nÓg, sometimes appearing in the mortal world. In one such case he sired Cúchulain, the great hero of Ulster. Lugh later appeared to his son during the Cattle Raid of Cooley, healing him over three days during battle.

• Other Mythology: Lugh is one of the most prominent Celtic deities, appearing in Britain and the European mainland as Lugus, or in Wales as Llew Llaw Gyffes. He is primarily associated with skill and rulership, but in some cases with light or the sun, and his title "of the Long Arm" is not uncommon.

Julius Caesar identified Lugus as the Roman god Mercury, a trickster and messenger of the gods, similar to Lugh's role before he became High King. In some of his attributes he is similar to the Norse deity Frey, god of fertility who had a boat that could change sizes and whose father is Njord, the god of the sea, like Lugh's foster-father Manannán mac Lir.

Chapter 5: The Morrigan

The Morrígan is the Irish goddess of death and destiny. Appearing just before all great battles as the goddess of fate, the Morrígan offers prophecy and favor to great heroes and gods alike. As the Phantom Queen, she circles the battlefield as a conspiracy of ravens to carry away the dead, She is at once a single deity and a triple goddess, made up of Ireland's most powerful goddesses.

Her husband is the Dagda, the Great God, who comes to her for prophecy before major battles. Several sacred sites across the Irish landscape honor her.

Who Is The Morrigan?

The Morrigan is the term given to Goddess Morrigan, one of the triple Goddesses in Celtic mythology. She represented the circle of life and was associated with both birth and death. Her name translates to "great queen" or "phantom ⬚ueen". She was a shape-shifter and looked over the rivers, fresh water and lakes. She is also described as being the patroness of revenge, magic, priestesses, night, prophecy and witches.

She is often depicted as a triple goddess but this varies by source. In Celtic mythology, the number three has incredible significance. At times, Morrigan is featured as one of three sisters while other times she is a singular figure.

Etymology

The Morrígan, sometimes simply Morrígan or Morrígu, is the anglicized form of the Gaelic Mór-Ríoghain. Scholars disagree about the exact etymology of this name, but have linked it to similar words across Europe, with Mór linked to a Proto-Indo-European word that means "terror" (which appears in English as part of the word "nightmare") and Ríoghain appearing as "ueen," similar to the Latin regina.

The Morrígan was seen by medieval Irish writers as an archetypal figure in her relation to spirits, particularly malevolent female spirits and monsters. These scholars referred to such spirits as morrígna. A particular example of this is the term morrígna being used as a way to describe the Middle Eastern lamia and demon-goddess Lilith from the Latin Vulgate Bible.

She is often called "Phantom Queen," a title acknowledging her relationship with the dead.

Attributes

The Morrígan is foremost a goddess of war and of death. She is also the goddess of prophecy and of fate, able to detail the future of all things, seeing as far as the end of the world. Thus is she all-knowing, and for a price, she can relay this information. What she prophesied is never wrong, and her wordings are exact, if poetic. Her appearance to royalty and to warriors can also represent whose side she favors in a battle. The raven's association with her stems from their appearance over battles, ready to feast on the dead.

She is a shapeshifter, appearing in different forms often in the same story. The most common of these is a shapely maiden, a warrior-queen prepared for battle, an old crone or hag, or a raven-observer of the events at hand. She can also change her shape to other animals beyond a raven, though less freuently, giving her the ability not just to see and know all things, but appear as them as well.

Her appearance at the deaths of prominent figures, such as those who fell at the Second Battle of Moytura or at the death of Cúchulain, has made many scholars link her to later spirits in Irish folklore such as the banshee, or "fairy woman." One clear example is her appearance to Cúchulain before his final battle, as an old woman cleaning blood off armor his armor.

Several locations are linked to the Morrígan by name. The most prominent is Fulacht na Mór Ríoghna ("cooking pit of the Morrígan") in County Tipperary. A fulacht fiadh, or a burned mound with a cooking pit, this Bronze Age site is linked to wandering bands of young warriors. A second location consists of two hills in County Meath, the Dá Chich na Morrigna, or the "two breasts" of the Morrígan, which may have served a ritual or guardianship capacity.

Triple Goddess

One of the most prominent aspects of the Morrígan is her nature as a triple goddess of war. In many stories, she appears as both an individual and as three different goddesses acting under a single name. She is one of many such figures in Irish and Celtic folklore, and world mythology at large. Membership within this triple goddess varies depending on the source. In some cases, the daughters of Ernmas, Badb, Macha, and Anand are named as the Morrígan, with Nemain or Fea sometimes replacing a goddess within this triad. Elsewhere, the Morrígan is listed as a sister of Badb and Macha, and Anand is simply an alternate name for her. This inconsistency likely represents early Irish scholars attempting to make sense of conflicting oral traditions.

Family

The Morrígan is the daughter of Ernmas, a mother-goddess and herself the daughter of

Nuada, king of the Tuatha Dé Danann. No father is given. Her siblings are Ériu, Banba, and Fódla, who make up the triple goddess representing the spirit and sovereignty of Ireland, as well as Badb and Macha, with whom the Morrígan make up a triple goddess of war. Her five brothers are the Glon, Gnim, Coscar, Fiacha, and Ollom.

She is married to the Dagda, the great god and chief of the Tuatha Dé Danann.

Mythology

• Origins: In Lebor Gabála Érenn the Morrígan appears as a member of the Tuatha Dé Danann, whose arrival in Ireland was met with resistance by earlier settlers of the island, the Firbolg, and the Fomorions. In the battles with the Firbolg, the Morrígan's mother perishes at the First Battle of Moytura, in County Galway, while her grandfather, King Nuada, loses a hand. Ultimately, they are victorious and establish a foothold on the island, securing their future but guaranteeing further conflict.

•   Cath Maig Tuired: The second threat, the monstrous Fomorions, proved more difficult. The new king, Lugh of the Long Arm, asked the Morrígan as to the outcome of this conflict. She predicted war. As the Tuatha Dé Danann prepared for battle against the Fomorions, the Dagda, a wise chief and god of magic and strategy, sought his wife the Morrígan for further prophecy. He found her at the ford of the River Unshin, in County Sligo, and there they made love. She gave her prophecy, that the Tuatha Dé Danann would be victorious, at a price. She also stated that she would slay the Fomorion king Indech, and bring two handfuls his blood and kidneys to the River Unshin.

On the day of battle, the gods gathered and prepared to fight the hordes of Fomorions at the Second Battle of Moytura, in County Sligo. Lugh asked the Morrígan what things she brought to the battle, to which each goddess replied: pursuit, death, and subjugation. The battle commenced and quickly turned to a bloodbath. Her grandfather Nuada was slain, and her husband the Dagda was mortally wounded.

At last the Morrígan joined the fray, ending the battle with her force and a poem. The Fomorion fled from the sight and sound of her and perished in the sea.

At the battle's end, the Morrígan celebrates their victory with a song, and as Badb, predicts that the world will end when the sea is without bounty and morals decay.

• Ulster Cycle: The Morrígan appears most prominently in the Ulster Cycle, where she appears only as a single individual, though in multiple forms. She both assists and antagonizes the hero of the cycle, Cúchulain.

In Táin Bó Regamna ("The Cattle Raid of Regamain"), Cúchulain chased an old woman driving a heifer from his territory, and insulted her. As he attacked her, she transformed into a raven, and Cúchulain, at last, realized that this is the mighty Morrígan, stating that if he had known who she was, he would have acted more wisely. She responded that no matter his actions, it would have ended in bad luck, and offered a prophecy as payment for his insults: he will die in an upcoming battle, and that she will be present.

Later, in Táin Bó Cúailnge ("The Cattle Raid of Cooley"), she appeared as a raven warning the Brown Bull of Cooley to flee before Queen Medb of Connacht. As Medb invades, the men of Ulster are inflicted with a terrible curse save one: Cúchulain, who alone defended the fords that mark the borders of Ulster. Between combat, a young maiden offered herself to Cúchulain as both lover and battle companion, an offer which he promptly rejected. As he began fighting Lóch mac Mofemis, Cúchulain found himself under attack by the forces of nature: an eel attempted to trip him, but he breaks its ribs; a wolf stampede cattle across the ford, but Cúchulain blinded the wolf in one eye with a sling; finally, the lead heifer of the stampede attacked, but her leg is broken by another stone from his sling.

Once he is victorious over Lóch, an old woman then appeared, milking a cow. Her eye is blinded, her leg broken, her ribs cracked. The old woman offered Cúchulain three drinks from her heifer, and after which he blessed her. These blessings heal each of her three wounds. Soon she revealed her true nature as the Morrígan. She then reminded Cúchulain of his previous insults, and that he swore never to offer her aid or heal her. He retorted that, had he known it was her, he would not have. Once more, she warns him of his fate.

Finally, the battle with Medb came to a head, and Cúchulain was offered an impossible situation: his geas required him not to eat dog meat, yet hospitality rules stated a gift cannot be refused. As forces gathered for battle, an old woman offered him dog meat, which he ate in hospitality, sealing his fate. Before battle he had a vision of an old woman cleaning blood from armor beside a river: his armor. The fighting began and he was mortally wounded, but vowed to die standing up. Using his exposed entrails, he wrapped himself to a stone, thus appearing alive. The tactic worked, stopping the forces of Legaid from attacking in fear of him. It is only when a single raven landed upon Cúchulain's shoulders that Lugaid and his men realized the truth. Despite her hatred of Cúchulain, the Morrígan favored the men of Ulster, who won the day.

• Other Mythologies: The Morrígan is found only in Ireland, but scholars have found similarities to other figures in Celtic lore. Most prominent is the great antagonist of Arthurian legend, Morgan le Fey, who shares many attributes with the Phantom Queen. Both are shapeshifters and prophets, appearing in many forms and foretelling the future with fearful accuracy. While some scholars link their two names, Morgan has a separate meaning in Welsh from the Irish Morrígan.

The Morrígan has no direct analogs in other regional mythologies but is similar to the Germanic Perchta and Odin in her relationship to ravens, death, and war.

Chapter 6: Beliefs, Practices, And Institutions

Cosmology and Eschatology

Little is known about the religious beliefs of the Celts of Gaul. They believed in a life after death, for they buried food, weapons, and ornaments with the dead. The druids, the early Celtic priesthood, taught the doctrine of transmigration of souls and discussed the nature and power of the gods. The Irish believed in an otherworld, imagined sometimes as underground and sometimes as islands in the sea. The otherworld was variously called "the Land of the Living," "Delightful Plain," and "Land of the Young" and was believed to be a country where there was no sickness, old age, or death, where happiness lasted forever, and a hundred years was as one day. It was similar to the Elysium of the Greeks and may have belonged to ancient Indo-European tradition. In Celtic eschatology, as noted in Irish vision or voyage tales, a beautiful girl approaches the hero and sings to him of this happy land. He follows her, and they sail away in a boat of glass and are seen no more; or else he returns after a short time to find that all his companions are dead, for he has really been away for hundreds of years. Sometimes the hero sets out on a quest, and a magic mist descends upon him. He finds himself before a palace and enters to find a warrior and a beautiful girl who make him welcome. The warrior may be Manannán, or Lugh himself may be the one who receives him, and after strange adventures the hero returns successfully. These Irish tales, some of which date from the 8th century, are infused with the magic quality that is found 400 years later in the Arthurian romances. Something of this quality is preserved, too, in the Welsh story of Branwen, daughter of Llŷr, which ends with the survivors of the great battle feasting in the presence of the severed head of Bran the Blessed, having forgotten all their suffering and sorrow. But this "delightful plain" was not accessible to all. Donn, god of the dead and ancestor of all the Irish, reigned over Tech Duinn, which was imagined as on or under Bull Island off the Beare Peninsula, and to him all men returned except the happy few.

Worship

According to Poseidonius and later classical authors Gaulish religion and culture were the concern of three professional classes— the druids, the bards, and between them an order closely associated with the druids that seems to have been best known by the Gaulish term vates, cognate with the Latin vates ("seers"). This threefold hierarchy had its reflex among the two main branches of Celts in Ireland and Wales but is best represented in early Irish tradition with its druids, filidh (singular fili), and bards; the filidh evidently correspond to the Gaulish vates.

The name druid means "knowing the oak tree" and may derive from druidic ritual, which seems in the early period to have been performed in the forest. Caesar stated that the druids avoided manual labour and paid no taxes, so that many were attracted by these privileges to join the order. They learned great numbers of verses by heart, and some studied for as long as 20 years; they thought it wrong to commit their learning to writing but used the Greek alphabet for other purposes.

As far as is known, the Celts had no temples before the Gallo-Roman period; their ceremonies took place in forest sanctuaries. In the Gallo-Roman period temples were erected, and many of them have been discovered by archaeologists in Britain as well as in Gaul.

Human sacrifice was practiced in Gaul: Cicero, Caesar, Suetonius, and Lucan all refer to it, and Pliny the Elder says that it occurred in Britain, too. It was forbidden under Tiberius and Claudius. There is some evidence that human sacrifice was known in Ireland and was forbidden by St. Patrick.

Festivals

Insular sources provide important information about Celtic religious festivals. In Ireland the year was divided into two periods of six months by the feasts of

Beltine (May 1) and Samhain (Samain; November 1), and each of these periods was equally divided by the feasts of Imbolc (February 1), and Lughnasadh (August 1). Samhain seems originally to have meant "summer," but by the early Irish period it had come to mark summer's end. Beltine is also called Cetśamain ("First Samhain"). Imbolc has been compared by the French scholar Joseph Vendryes to the Roman lustrations and apparently was a feast of purification for the farmers. It was sometimes called oímelc ("sheep milk") with reference to the lambing season. Beltine ("Fire of Bel") was the summer festival, and there is a tradition that on that day the druids drove cattle between two fires as a protection against disease. Lughnasadh was the feast of the god Lugh.

The impact of Christianity

The conversion to Christianity had inevitably a profound effect on this socio-religious system from the 5th century onward, though its character can only be extrapolated from documents of considerably later date. By the early 7th century the church had succeeded in relegating the druids to ignominious irrelevancy, while the filidh, masters of traditional learning, operated in easy harmony with their clerical counterparts, contriving at the same time to retain a considerable part of their pre-Christian tradition, social status, and privilege. But virtually all the vast corpus of early vernacular literature that has survived was written down in monastic scriptoria, and it is part of the task of modern scholarship to identify the relative roles of traditional continuity and ecclesiastical innovation as reflected in the written texts. Cormac's Glossary (c. 900) recounts that St. Patrick banished those mantic rites of the filidh that involved offerings to demons, and it seems probable that the church took particular pains to stamp out animal sacrifice and other rituals grossly repugnant to Christian teaching. What survived of ancient ritual practice tended to be related to filidhecht, the traditional repertoire of the filidh, or to the central institution of sacral kingship.

Chapter 7: Remnants Of Gaulish And Other Mythology

The Celts also worshipped a number of deities of which we know little more than their names. Classical writers preserve a few fragments of legends or myths that may possibly be Celtic.

According to the Syrian rhetorician Lucian, Ogmios was supposed to lead a band of men chained by their ears to his tongue as a symbol of the strength of his eloquence.

The Roman poet Lucan (1st century AD) mentions the gods Taranis, Teutates and Esus, but there is little Celtic evidence that these were important deities.

A number of objets d'art, coins, and altars may depict scenes from lost myths, such as the representations of Tarvos Trigaranus or of an equestrian 'Jupiter' surmounting a snake-legged human-like figure. The Gundestrup cauldron has been also interpreted mythically.

Along with dedications giving us god names, there are also deity representations to which no name has yet been attached. Among these are images of a three headed or three faced god, a squatting god, a god with a snake, a god with a wheel, and a horseman with a kneeling giant. Some of these images can be found in Late Bronze Age peat bogs in Britain, indicating the symbols were both pre-Roman and widely spread across Celtic culture.

• Perhaps it was some of the latter: Returning home as rich mercenaries, merchants, or slaves stolen from Britain or Gaul, that first brought the Christian faith to Ireland. Some early sources claim that there were missionaries active in southern Ireland long before St. Patrick. Whatever the route, and there were probably many, this new faith was to have the most profound effect on the Irish.

• Tradition maintains that in AD 432: St. Patrick arrived on the island and, in the years that followed, worked to convert the Irish to Christianity. On the other hand, according to Prosper of Aquitaine, a contemporary chronicler, Palladius was sent to Ireland by the Pope in 431 as "first Bishop to the Irish believing in Christ", which demonstrates that there were already Christians living in Ireland. Palladius seems to have worked purely as Bishop to Irish Christians in the Leinster and Meath kingdoms, while Patrick who may have arrived as late as 461 worked first and foremost as a missionary to the Pagan Irish, converting in the more remote kingdoms located in Ulster and Connacht.

• Patrick is traditionally credited: With preserving the tribal and social patterns of the Irish, codifying their laws and changing only those that conflicted with Christian practices. He is also credited with introducing the Roman alphabet, which enabled Irish monks to preserve parts of the extensive Celtic oral literature. The historicity of these claims remains the subject of debate and there is no direct evidence linking Patrick with any of these accomplishments. The myth of Patrick, as scholars refer to it, was developed in the centuries after his death.

• The druid tradition collapsed: First in the face of the spread of the new faith, and ultimately in the aftermath of famine and plagues due to the climate changes of 535–536. Irish scholars excelled in the study of Latin learning and Christian theology in the monasteries that flourished shortly thereafter. Missionaries from Ireland to England and Continental Europe spread news of the flowering of learning, and scholars from other nations came to Irish monasteries. The excellence and isolation of these monasteries helped preserve Latin learning during the Early Middle Ages. The period of Insular art, mainly in the fields of illuminated manuscripts, metalworking, and sculpture flourished and produced such treasures as the Book of Kells, the Ardagh Chalice, and the many carved stone crosses that dot the island. Insular style was to be a crucial ingredient in the formation of the Romanesque and Gothic styles throughout Western Europe. Sites dating to this period include clochans, ringforts and promontory forts.

• The first English involvement in Ireland took place in this period: In 684 AD an English expeditionary force sent by Northumbrian King Ecgfrith invaded Ireland in the summer of that year. The English forces managed to seize a number of captives and booty, but they apparently did not stay in Ireland for long. The next English involvement in Ireland would take place a little more than half a millennium later in 1169 AD when the Normans invaded the country.

Gaulish god

The Gaulish god "Mars" illustrates vividly the difficulty of equating individual Roman and Celtic deities. A famous passage in Lucan's Bellum civile mentions the bloody sacrifices offered to the three Celtic gods Teutates, Esus, and Taranis; of two later commentators on Lucan's text, one identifies Teutates with Mercury, the other with Mars. The probable explanation of this apparent confusion, which is paralleled elsewhere, is that the Celtic gods are not rigidly compartmentalized in terms of function. Thus "Mercury" as the god of sovereignty may function as a warrior, while "Mars" may function as protector of the tribe, so that either one may plausibly be equated with Teutates.

The problem of identification is still more pronounced in the case of the Gaulish "Apollo," for some of his 15 or more epithets may refer to separate deities. The solar connotations of Belenus (from Celtic: bel, "shining" or "brilliant") would have supported the identification with the Greco-Roman Apollo. Several of his epithets, such as Grannus and Borvo (which are associated etymologically with the notions of "boiling" and "heat," respectively), connect him with healing and especially with the therapeutic powers of thermal and other springs, an area of religious belief that retained much of its ancient vigour in Celtic lands throughout the Middle Ages and even to the present time. Maponos ("Divine Son" or "Divine Youth") is attested in Gaul but occurs mainly in northern Britain. He appears in medieval Welsh literature as Mabon, son of Modron (that is, of Matrona, "Divine Mother"), and he evidently figured in a myth of the infant god carried off from his mother when three nights old. His name survives in Arthurian romance under the forms Mabon, Mabuz, and Mabonagrain. His Irish equivalent was Mac ind Óg ("Young

Son" or "Young Lad"), known also as Oenghus, who dwelt in Bruigh na Bóinne, the great Neolithic, and therefore pre-Celtic, passage grave of Newgrange (or Newgrange House). He was the son of Dagda (or Daghda), chief god of the Irish, and of Boann, the personified sacred river of Irish tradition. In the literature the Divine Son tends to figure in the role of trickster and lover.

Chapter 8: Julius Caesar On Celtic Religion And Their Meaning

Celtic Religion, Religious Beliefs And Practices Of The Ancient Celts

The Celts, an ancient Indo-European people, reached the apogee of their influence and territorial expansion during the 4th century BC, extending across the length of Europe from Britain to Asia Minor. From the 3rd century BC onward their history is one of decline and disintegration, and with Julius Caesar's con?uest of Gaul (58–51 BC) Celtic independence came to an end on the European continent. In Britain and Ireland this decline moved more slowly, but traditional culture was gradually eroded through the pressures of political subjugation; today the Celtic languages are spoken only on the western periphery of Europe, in restricted areas of Ireland, Scotland, Wales, and Brittany (in this last instance largely as a result of immigration from Britain from the 4th to the 7th century AD). It is not surprising, therefore, that the unsettled and uneven history of the Celts has affected the documentation of their culture and religion.

Caesar on the Celtic Deities

Caesar, who tries to fit the Gallic religion into the framework of Roman mythology - which was exactly what the Gauls themselves did after the conquest - says they held Mercury to be the chief of the gods, and looked upon him as the inventor of all the arts, as the presiding deity of commerce, and as the guardian of roads and guide of travellers. One may conjecture that he was particularly, to the Gauls as to the Romans the guide of the dead, of travellers to the Other-world, Many bronze statues to Mercury, of Gaulish origin. still remain, the name being adopted by the Gauls, as many place-names still testify. Mont Mercure, Mercoeur; Mercoirey, Montmartre Apollo was regarded as the deity of medicine and healing, Minerva was the initiator of arts and crafts, Jupiter governed the sky, and Mars presided over war. Caesar is here, no doubt, classifying under five types and by

Roman names a large number of Gallic divinities.

Sources

Two main types of sources provide information on Celtic religion: the sculptural monuments associated with the Celts of continental Europe and of Roman Britain, and the insular Celtic literatures that have survived in writing from medieval times. Both pose problems of interpretation. Most of the monuments, and their accompanying inscriptions, belong to the Roman period and reflect a considerable degree of syncretism between Celtic and Roman gods; even where figures and motifs appear to derive from pre-Roman tradition, they are difficult to interpret in the absence of a preserved literature on mythology. Only after the lapse of many centuries— beginning in the 7th century in Ireland, even later in Wales—was the mythological tradition consigned to writing, but by then Ireland and Wales had been Christianized and the scribes and redactors were monastic scholars. The resulting literature is abundant and varied, but it is much removed in both time and location from its epigraphic and iconographic correlatives on the Continent and inevitably reflects the redactors' selectivity and something of their Christian learning. Given these circumstances it is remarkable that there are so many points of agreement between the insular literatures and the continental evidence. This is particularly notable in the case of the Classical commentators from Poseidonius (c. 135–c. 51 BC) onward who recorded their own or others' observations on the Celts.

Chapter 9: The Gallo-Roman Deities

Regarding the Celtic pantheon, let's start by saying that the Celts worshiped a multitude of gods and goddesses, although these differed according to the nation of origin. The Irish worshiped deities other than the Gallic ones, who themselves were different from the Gaelic ones. Another point to consider is that not only were the gods known by different names but also that many of these names were considered too sacred to be pronounced aloud. It is important to remember that in pre-Christian times, people worshiped complex and imperfect deities, who, like men, had their own personalities, interests, and feelings. For this reason, a "professional" religious was absolutely necessary, capable of knowing all these things and able to avoid their anger, which would seriously endanger the health of the whole tribe. Because the gods were similar to men in nature and temperament, they were much more accessible than men themselves. The idea that the gods are the architects of man's morality and judgment was a concept foreign to most of the European populations of the time.

Mercury: The Inventor of All the Arts

The Gauls paid the highest cult to a god that the Romans identified with Mercury. Despite the abundance of dedications and monuments that the Gauls raised to their Mercury in late ancient times and the large number of epithets attributed to him, the original identity of this important Celtic deity continues to elude us.

The god that the Gauls worship above all others is Mercury. This news might be surprising to a Roman citizen, who knows well that it is Jupiter, the king of the gods, who must be given the supreme cult. Evidently, the Gauls do not think so, as Caesar testified in the commentaries on his campaigns. The image that these barbarians have of Mercury does not differ much from ours. Also in Gaul, Mercury is the god who shows the way to travelers, who guides and protects them along the roads, and who takes care of trade and financial activities.

He is the most able to ensure good earnings. It is also to Mercury that the Gauls attribute the invention of all the arts and techniques. The Gauls raise the greatest number of monuments to Mercury, such is the devotion they bring to him. This devotion (pietas) was noticed by Caesar at the time of his campaigns but, still today, the traveler who crosses the Gauls can easily see, along the roads, the many statues and inscriptions dedicated to the god of travelers and artisans. Since they were Romanized, the Gauls have taken to represent Mercury according to the classic image: a young naked man with a shaved beard, with a caduceus in his hand, a petasus on his head, sandals on his feet, and a purse for money in his hand. However, if necessary, one can encounter very different images of a Mercury, dressed in the Gallic style, with a bearded chin. Sometimes animals accompany him: a rooster, a goat, a lizard, or a tortoise. A Greek may perhaps recognize in the tortoise the one from which the very young Hermes drew his first lyre, but the rooster and the goat remain symbols completely foreign to the classical figurations of the god. Other times, next to Mercury we find a snake with ram horns. Mercury is often joined by a goddess called Rosmerta, the "provident". The Romans identify her with Maia, Fortuna, Felicitas, and Salus. The Gauls also call her Visucia, the "wise one". In the city of Lugdunum, which the Romans made the capital of Gaul, the cult of Mercury is particularly cared for and placed in close relationship with that of the emperor Augustus.

The traveler who crosses the Gauls, admiring the numerous monuments that the Gauls have dedicated to Mercury and stopping to read the dedications, will notice how many and which epithets, both Celtic and Latin, the god is called and invoked in those lands. Some of these names are widespread, while others attest to small local cults. It is difficult to say how many of these epithets are actually addressed to the supreme god of the Gauls, Mercury, the inventor of all the arts, and which ones conceal other deities that, for some reason, have come to be identified with the Roman god. These names have different meanings and different origins. Many of them are simple epithets of Gallo-Roman Mercury, some of Celtic origin, others purely Latin. Some of these epithets are evidently related to local cults of various tribes. Among these names, there are also those of Gallic divinities in their own right that have been identified with the Roman Mercury: the case of Cissonius, a god worshiped by the Treveri, but also known in Aquitaine, and of Gebrinius, a god of the Germanic tribe of the Ubii. The list also contains the names of two great Gallic deities, Esus and Teutates, which our theologians have identified with both Mercury and Mars.

Mercury is not only the supreme god of all the Gauls but also the protector of many individual tribes. One of the many Gallic names of Mercury is Teutates, "father of the tribe" (although some associate this name with Mars). In fact, Mercury sometimes assumes the appearance of a warrior god and, as such, watches over the territory of the tribe and safeguards its borders. Defensor and Finitimus are precisely two Latin names that the Gauls willingly associate with Mercury in his aspect of tribal god. Very devoted to Mercury are the

Segusiavi, whose city Lugdunum was founded under the auspices of the god. The Arverni, who worship Mercury in a temple erected on Mount Domus, are considered particularly close to the god. However, many Gallic tribes worship Mercury on mountaintops. Mediomatrici and Leuci, for example, worship Mercury Clavariates on the peaks of Vosges. With the same name, the god is known by the Lingones and the Tricasses. Mediomatrixes worship a Mercury Vosegus. Mercury Vellaunus, the "valiant", is adored with this epithet throughout Gaul, but above all by the Vellauni tribe. He is also a warrior god, so much so that in Britain one speaks rather of a Mars Vellaunus. In Belgic Gaul, the Treveri identified Mercury with their god Cissonius. However, the Gallic cult of Mercury is also boundless among the Germanic peoples who live on the two banks of the Rhine. Mercury Visucius, the "wise man", is the name by which the god is known in Superior Germany. The Cimbri, people of Germanic origin, although Celtized, worship a Mercury Cimbrianus or Cimbrius. The same can be said for the border Germans: The Ubii identify their god Gebrinius with Mercury. The Nemetes likewise address a Mercury Seno. Yet even the Germans, as confirmed by Publius Cornelius Tacitus, see Mercury as a supreme god.

Particularly devoted to Mercury is the tribe of the Arverni, who have always had a particular bond with the god, so much so that throughout Gaul, right up to the limes of the Rhine, it is customary to invoke Mercury Arvernus, as if the god belonged to the Arverni, or rather, as if a holier and deeper cult was rendered to their Mercury. Elsewhere, he is invoked as Arvernorix, "king of the Arverni". The Arverni have dedicated a famous temple to Mercury, erected on the top of Mount Domus (the Puy-de-Dôm), shining with precious marble and with a lead-covered roof. Here is the imposing bronze statue of Mercury Dumiatis. It was forged under the reign of Emperor Lucius Domitius Nero, the famous Greek sculptor and toreutics Zenodorus, who worked on it for ten years and received a salary of forty million sesterces from the Arverni. The statue, more than 100 feet (30 meters) high, portrays the god crouched on a stone; he is depicted according to classical models, naked, with a winged petasus on his head and a purse for money. At his feet are a rooster, a goat, and a turtle. This statue is so well known among the Gauls that they made many small copies of it, which they keep for devotion. After giving such a fine proof of his talent, Zenodorus was summoned to Rome by Nero, and there he outdid himself by making the 119-foot-tall colossus representing the emperor.

Among the numerous epithets that the Gauls have attributed to Mercury, there are two—Mercury Moccus and Mercury Artaius—in which the god is close to two animals: the pig and the bear. Such epithets may perhaps surprise us, but they should not lead us to hasty accusations of impiety. For the Celts, the pig (moccos) is a symbol of wisdom, as it feeds on acorns and hazelnuts, fruits of trees that the druids consider sacred because they are associated with deep and occult knowledge. The cult of Mercury Moccus is particularly felt by the people of the Lingones, in whose capital, Andematunum, one can admire dedications and monuments devoted to this curious porcine Mercury. The bear (artos) is, for the Celts, a noble beast—a symbol of strength and royalty. Many Gallic personal names refer to this animal: Articnos, Artomagus, Arctorix. And because the bear cuts down the hives and feeds on the honey distilled by bees, it is perhaps related to the idea of immortality. The Celts believe that the gods drink a special mead that keeps them eternally young. The cult of Mercury Artaius is widespread among the Allobroges, settled along the Rhodanus River; monuments dedicated to him are found in the cities of Gallia Narbonensis and Cularo (today Grenoble). But this is not the only cult that the Celts dedicate to the bear. In Britain, the bear-god Matunus is worshiped and may be the local equivalent of Mercury Artaius. The goddess Arduinna is depicted riding a boar. The Helvetii instead worship Artio, the goddess of bears.

The streets of Magna Graecia are lined with images dedicated to Hermes, called "herms". Even in Gaul, images of Mercury are placed along the streets. These images may have marked phallic characteristics. The Belgae sometimes present a curious

Mercury with three penises, the second on the nose and the third on the top of the head. Thus, they combine the magical meaning of triplicity with the symbolism of fertility and luck traditionally linked to the phallus.

In many images, Mercury is accompanied by a female figure. Sometimes this goddess is defined with a Roman name: It can be Maia, the mother of the god, or Fortuna, Felicitas, Diana, Salus, or Minerva. However, it often bears the Gallic name of Rosmerta, the "great dispenser". The cult of the divine couple formed by Mercury and Rosmerta is practiced in most of the Gallo-Roman regions, but is particularly widespread in central and eastern Gaul, along the Rhone, Meuse, and Moselle rivers, and on both banks of the Rhine. The tribes of Lingones, Treveri, Mediomatrici, and Leuci are devoted to Rosmerta. In the figurations, Rosmerta is usually standing and holding a cornucopia or a bag. She often has the caduceus, like her companion Mercury, with whom she forms a couple aimed at material profits and distributions. The Gauls invoke her so that prosperity will favor them and so that they will never remain without anything. The divine couple is even worshiped in Britain, where Rosmerta is represented with a wooden bucket and ladle. There are temples dedicated to them among the Dobunni, and some of these temples are found in the Roman colonies. Another place of worship dedicated to Mercury and Rosmerta is located in Aquae Sulis. Variants of the name of Rosmerta are Atesmerta and Cantismerta. All these names contain a Celtic root whose meaning is "to dispense"; the same one is found in the name of Adsmerius or Atesmertus, with which Mercury is honored among the Lingones tribe. Thus, Adsmerius and Rosmerta, or, with still closer correlation, Atesmerius and Atesmerta, come to be the "dispensing god" and the "dispensing goddess". At other times, Mercury and his companion are instead called Visucius and Visucia, the "wise man" and the "wise woman", again with a perfect symmetry of roles and attributes.

We have so far talked about the god to whom the Gauls attribute the supreme cult and who in Roman times was identified with

Mercury. However, we don't know the original Gallic name of this god. Identification problems are quite complex. For example, the gods Teutates and Esus have both been associated with both Mercury and Mars. It is suspected that our informants did not have very clear ideas! So, what was the Gallic name of Mercury? Some say it is Lugos, the "shining one". This name, as far as we know, is never attested to in the epigraphies or in the surveys of our writers, but many localities scattered in Gaul, in Germany, in Britain, and even in Hispania—places often sacred to Mercury—have a name that derives from a "Lugos". One of these is precisely the city of Lugdunum, which in the time of Augustus became the capital of all Gauls.

On a hill, not far from the place where the Rhodanus and Arar rivers mix their waters, stands the city of Lugdunum. At first the center of the Segusiavi tribe, Lugudunum then became, in Roman times, the political, cultural, and religious capital of all the Gauls, who gather here in their assemblies, the Concilia Galliarum. It is a beautiful and populous city, located in a pleasant place, from which one can enjoy a wonderful view of the Alps. It is also a large commercial emporium and the Roman governors have gold and silver coins minted there. It is said that this place got its name when two Gaulish chiefs, Atepomaros and Momoros, arrived there. Driven out by Seseroneos, they came here, obeying the order of an oracle, to found a city there. Ditches were being dug for the foundations when a flock of crows appeared. The birds fluttered over them and covered the trees. Momoros, an expert in the science of augur, called the new city Lugdunum, because—the Hellenic authors say—in the Celtic language, the crow is called lugos and a fortified place dunum. As evidence of these facts, medallions were wrought depicting the god of the city with a crow at his feet. However, it must be said that the Greeks are wrong: "crow" in Gallic is not lugos, but brennos. Indeed, Lugdunum means "shining fortress" or, perhaps, "fortress of the shining (god)". Later, the emperor Augustus, in placing a capital at the center of the now subjugated Gaul, chose Lugdunum. Facing the city, at the confluence of the two rivers, the Gauls wanted to dedicate a magnificent sanctuary to Augustus. There, they placed a splendid altar on which they wrote the names of the 60 Gallic tribes and placed a statue for each tribe. When the emperor wanted to place his annual feast, the Feriae Augusti, he chose as a recurrence the first of August, the day that, to the Gauls, was sacred to Mercury.

In Hispania, the Celtiberians worship the Lugoves gods, patrons of shoemakers. Is it a plural form of the god Lugos plus several protectors of this profession? We do not know. Mercury was certainly the inventor of every technique, and therefore could also be the inventor of shoemaking.

Jupiter Taranis: The God with the Wheel

The Gauls considered him the king of the gods, and the Romans did not take long to identify him with Jupiter. His Celtic name was likely Taranis, the lord of thunder, and his image that of the "god with the wheel".

The place that the Gauls reserve for Jupiter is curious. They consider him the king of the gods, but they do not give him great importance in myth and worship. Caesar testified to this in the commentaries on his campaigns. Citing the five main Gallic gods, Caesar says that Mercury is the god whom the Gauls worship above all others and that only after him do Apollo, Mars, Jupiter, and Minerva follow. It may seem bizarre that these barbarians assign a secondary place to the lord and master of all the gods, but this should not lead us to consider the Gauls ignorant in terms of religion—a subject in which, indeed, they appear to be very versed. The minor importance that they assign to Jupiter is not to be considered impiety, but a different approach to the spheres of the sacred. Much revered from Gaul to Hispania, from Helvetia to Noricum, the Celtic Jupiter does not differ much from ours. He is a heavenly god in his most sublime and terrifying aspect, but also a god of thunder and life-giving rain. His sacred tree is the oak, and even in this, the Gauls agree with the Greeks and Romans. Since the Gauls have been subdued, Jupiter is represented with the usual classical attributes: the scepter, the lightning bolt, and the eagle. Typically Gallic, on the other hand, is the wheel that the god carries with him, which he sometimes holds, and which at other times he seems to lean on. This wheel, which has a variable number of spokes, perhaps represents the thunder rumbling in the clouds.

The Gauls have not attributed many epithets to Jupiter, their king of the gods, above all compared to all those attributed to Mercury or Mars. Of these epithets, some are of Gallic origin; among these, the name Taranis, the "thunderer", is very important. The Gauls have drawn other epithets from the Roman cult, such as the one, well known in the Romanized areas, of Jupiter Optimus Maximus.

We do not know the exact name of the Gallic Jupiter, but many think it is Taranis, the "thunderer". With this name, Jupiter is worshiped throughout the Celtic territory: in Gaul, in Britain, and in Germany. Along the Rhine, the god is known by the name of Jupiter Taranucnus. There are traces of a cult of Jupiter Taranucnus even in distant Dalmatia. Taranis is the lord of thunder, whose rumble is evoked by his own name, and as such has power over him among the powers of heaven. Storms and bad weather come from him. From him comes the rain, which brings fertility and abundance. The poet Lucan states that sacrifices no less ferocious than those that the Scythians give to Diana take place on the Taranis altar. His scholiasts add that the Gauls consider Taranis a god similar to Jupiter, lord of wars and maximum of the gods, but also similar to Dis Pater, god of darkness and death. When Taranis has the appearance of Jupiter, he is appeased by the sacrifice of human lives to him in bloody rites. When he looks like Dis Pater, his victims are burned alive in large wooden vats. Caesar also agreed that some Gallic peoples sacrificed numerous human victims burnt alive in large vats or wooden simulacra. However, with the Christianization of the Gauls, these barbarian customs partially ceased and the Gauls began to replace men with animals in their sacrifices. Even today, in fact, the custom of making large bonfires remains among them, with dogs, cats, foxes, and other animals, enclosed in wooden or wicker baskets, thrown on them.

In Cisalpine Gaul, Jupiter was worshiped on the peaks at the top of the mountains. For this, he was called Poeninus, the god of the peaks. In the year 218 BC, the leader Hannibal, at the head of the imposing Carthaginian army, crossed the Alps and descended from Gaul to Italy, threatening the power of Rome on its own territory. The Second Punic War reached its most dramatic moment. Two centuries later, however, Roman historians were still debating which Alpine pass the Carthaginians had passed through, and there was a tendency to indicate a certain passage near Mons Poeninus (Mount Pennino). Indeed, it was thought that this mountain had taken its name from the Poeni, or the Carthaginians themselves. Titus Livius, in his historical work, refutes this argument. If Hannibal had taken the Poeninus pass, he would not have reached the territory of the Taurini Celts, as he later did. In reality, says Livius, the origin of the name of the mountain is different, as the Celtic tribe of Seduni Veragri, which inhabited those mountains, knew well. Indeed, they traced the name of the

Pennine Alps not to the passage of the Carthaginians but to the god they worshiped on the highest peak of those mountains—a god that the Romans identified with Jupiter and Silvanus, but which they called Poeninus, the lord of the peaks.

Sometimes the Gauls refer to Jupiter with the epithet of Baginatis, god of oaks. And, in fact, the Celtic people, who still have great respect for all trees, consider the oaks to be particularly sacred. Apparently, they worship Jupiter precisely in the image of an oak. However, this is nothing new. Many peoples worship the god of thunder in oak and beech, especially when the tree is struck by lightning—the Thracians and the Germans, for example. However, the Greeks and Romans also believe that the oak is the sacred tree to Jupiter.

We do not know of any myth concerning the Gallic Jupiter. One of them, however, seems to be suggested by certain pillars and columns widespread in many places in the Celtic area: among the Lingones, the Treveri, the Arverni, and especially in the Rhine valley, but also among the Helvetii and even in Britain. At the top of a high column stands the image of a god on horseback, standing above a bearded giant with a snake or fish tail: The Anguiped lies on the ground, its face contorted with terror, crushed under the hooves of the horse. In other cases, the god is standing erect and the monster is lying at his feet. The god is armed; he often wields a javelin or a flash of lightning, but at other times he holds the wheel, and only for this reason can he be identified with Jupiter. What history, myth, or symbolism is the basis of this figure, we do not know.

Sucellus: The God with the Mallet

Progenitor of the Gauls, he was a god in which the Romans saw Dis Pater, lord of the dead and king of the underworld. This divinity may be identified in the images of the so-called "god with mallet", whose Gallic name was Sucellus.

Caesar states, in a passage of his commentaries, that the Gauls claim to be descendants of Dis Pater, the lord of the underworld, and add that this was handed down to them by the wisdom of the druids. This is also why they do not calculate time by counting days, but nights; Christmas dates and the beginning of the months and years are counted by making the day begin with the night. According to the Gauls, Dis Pater is the progenitor of humanity—the first man to be born, but also the first to die, and as such, he became the lord of the underworld. In his honor, the Gauls practice human sacrifices, burning men alive in wooden vats. The inscriptions and dedications to Dis Pater come from southern Germany and the northwestern Balkans. The god appears next to his wife Erecura, whom the Romans consider a local form of Proserpina and who has the emblems of the great mother.

When Caesar speaks of the Gallic Dis Pater, he is perhaps referring to the "god with the mallet", whom the Gauls call Sucellus, "the good hitter" or "he who strikes well". The cult of Sucellus has its center in Gallia Narbonensis, in the Rhodanus and Sauconna valley, where it is revered by the Vocontii,

Allobroges, and Sequani tribes. From here, his cult goes north; Sucellus is well known and revered in Belgic Gaul and in Superior Germany. Traces of his cult can even be found in distant Britain. In the figurations that the Gauls make of this deity, Sucellus appears as a mature man, mild-looking, with a thick, curly beard and hair. He is dressed in the Gallic manner, in simple, peasant clothes: a tunic tight at the waist and sandals on his feet. In his left hand, he holds a long shaft, one end of which points to the ground, while the other, higher than the god's head, ends in a large mallet. Some have described it as a hammer or maul, but then the handle would have been shorter and sturdier. Rather, Sucellus appears to be holding it like a scepter, giving an impression of calm royalty rather than strength. On the right, the god carries a small vase similar to an olla, which seems to serve as a symbol of wealth and fertility. In other and different figurations, Sucellus holds a falx or money bag. In other figurations, widespread above all in Alesia, he appears leaning against a large vat. The goddess Nantosuelta often accompanies

Sucellus, as dignified and regal as her consort. Very often, Sucellus is escorted by a small dog or, sometimes, by a crow.

The Romans identified Sucellus with Hercules, but also and above all with Silvanus, the Roman god of the woods and agriculture. With this name, the god is honored throughout the Celtic area but seems to have the center of his cult in Gallia Narbonensis. In Britain, Silvanus is equated with various local deities; along Hadrian's Wall, he is honored as the god of hunting, and his name is sometimes added to that of Sucellus. Still, in Britain, he is invoked as Silvanus Callirius, the "king of the hazelnut forest", and deer seem to be sacred to him. The Gallic Silvanus retains the typical attributes of Sucellus: a mallet higher than his head, which he holds majestically in his left hand, and the small olla, which he holds out with his right hand. These attributes—the mallet and the vase—also appear alone in the commemorative plaques dedicated to Silvanus. In the role of Silvanus, Sucellus has a somewhat different appearance: He wears only a short tunic of skin, perhaps of a wolf, which leaves his legs and right shoulder uncovered, and on his head is a crown of laurel leaves. Attributes of the Gallic Silvanus (besides the mallet and the vase) can be fruit trees, flutes, knives, and axes. He is sometimes depicted with a falx in his hand, indicating the domestication of the wilderness.

In Gaul, a few epithets are attributed to Silvanus, which we report here: Callirius, Cocidius, Sinquatis, Sucellus, Vinotonus, "god of wine". In particular, Callirius and Vinotonus were widespread among the Britons and Sinquatis among the Belgians.

It should be noted, however, that some of these epithets Silvanus has in common with other deities. For example, Cocidius is elsewhere an epithet of Mars.

In other places, the "god with the mallet" appears in a third, completely different aspect. He is naked, with a wolf skin draped across his back and arm. In some cases, five minor mallets seem to branch out from his mallet, in a sort of emanation and multiplication of divine power. Here, the "god with a mallet" can be identified with Pluto or Dis Pater, who, for the Romans, is the god of the dead but whom the Gauls consider the father of their race. The bride of this Gallic Pluto is Proserpina or Erecura. A three-headed dog often accompanies them.

A goddess with a majestic and regal bearing often appears next to Sucellus, dressed in a long tunic, according to Roman custom. Her name is Nantosuelta, the lady of the sunny valleys. She holds a cornucopia, or sometimes a small patera. At the Raurici, she holds a long shaft surmounted by a sort of fanum. The Romans identified her with Diana. When Sucellus has the appearance of Dis Pater, his companion's name is Erecura, although, of course, the Romans call her Proserpina.

Apollo: The God of Light and Water

The Romans indistinctly identified with Apollo a host of different Gallic deities, associated with light and spring waters, linked to thermal centers and able to heal from all diseases. Grannus, Borvo, and Belenus were some of them.

In second place among the five main Gallic gods, Caesar mentions Apollo, and says of him that he hunts down disease. We can imagine Caesar's perplexity in front of this Gallic Apollo—so similar to the Apollo that centuries earlier the Romans had derived from the Etruscans and then from the Greeks, yet so inextricably different. In Rome, Apollo was never a very important god; instead, the Gauls hold him in the highest regard. His cult, very ancient and rooted, is widespread in even the most peripheral areas of the Celtic area. While the Greek Apollo is known for spreading diseases and plagues with arrow shots, the Gauls see, in Apollo, a divinity linked to the brightness of the light and the transparency of the waters, a healing god with great healing abilities. The great feast of May 1st is dedicated to him; during it, the Gauls light large fires to welcome summer, but also to hunt diseases and purify livestock. Horses are sacred to Apollo, as they are animals traditionally linked to the cult of the solar chariot. However, it cannot be generalized, as Apollo became, after the Roman conquest, a generic name that covers many different yet similar divinities, generally related to thermal springs and their healing powers. Belenus, Grannus, and Borvo are just some of these gods with similar shades, identified with Apollo. An infinity of temples have been dedicated to these "Apollos" throughout Gaul, and for the most part, they are located near the springs and thermal springs. Some of these temples are very large and pilgrims from all over Gaul meet there. In these places, Apollo is worshiped with a large number of names and epithets and is often flanked by a consort goddess with whom he forms a divine couple. Pilgrims bring, to Apollo, images depicting sick body parts, for which they hope for a quick recovery: hands and feet, internal organs, breasts, and genitals. The Apollo Vindonnus of the Lingons, for example, specializes in eye care; he is presented with images of hands offering fruit and bread. In these temples is an abaton or dormitory, with many small cubicles in which pilgrims retire to sleep, hoping that the god appears to them in a dream to heal them. Skilled doctors and priests are consecrated to the god.

Many different Gallic deities, especially if related to light and thermal waters, were identified with the classical god Apollo—so much so that today it is not easy, in analyzing the many epithets to which Apollo has been referred in Gallic countries, to distinguish which of these hide the names of small local deities later identified with the Greek-Roman god, or which of them were actually epithets of the great Apollo Celtic of which Caesar spoke.

Grannus is a god linked to the sun and the thermal springs, to which great healing powers are attributed. Identified with Apollo, he is worshiped in the vast region between the Seine and the Rhine, especially by the Lingoni and Treveri tribes, and then even farther north, in the upper course of the Rhine. Among the various centers dedicated to him is the thermal town of Aachen, which later became the capital of the kingdom of the Franks. However, his cult also extends to other regions: to the northwest, toward Armorica and then to Britain, and to the southeast, along the course of the Danube, up to Szőny in Hungary. Grannus' bond with the sun is very strong. The Treveri call him Phœbus and in figures, they put him at the helm of the solar chariot. Grannus is well known as a healing god and his fame has extended far beyond the Celtic world. In his temples and shrines, pilgrims can purify themselves in sacred waters; after making offerings and praying to the god, they enter the dormitories, hoping that the god will appear to them in sleep. At his peak of popularity, Grannus was worshiped even in Rome. In 215, the emperor Caracalla, who fell ill, visited the temples of the Gallic god Grannus, the Greco-Roman god Asclepius, and the Egyptian god Serapis, hoping to recover from his illness. However, despite all his efforts, he did not get what he hoped for. The wife of Grannus is Sirona, the goddess of the stars. Generally represented with fruit or spikes in hand, but also with a crescent on the forehead, or holding a snake symbol of regeneration on the arm, she is closely associated with Grannus. Her cult has its center between the Rhine and the Upper Moselle.

Another god identified with Apollo and linked to the thermal waters is Borvo, the boiling one. His name is linked to ancient thermal towns, as well as to many waterways. It is especially worshiped in central Gaul, in a band that includes the tribes of the Arverni, the Aedui, the Lingoni, and the Treveri. Paredra (the one who sits behind) of Borvo is the goddess Ritona, the goddess of fords and waterways, who is especially adored by the Treveri. However, the Lingons attribute, as his wife, the goddess Damona, who elsewhere is associated with Apollo Moritasgus or Albius. Elsewhere, the god and his paredra are called Bormanus and Bormana.

Many of the Gallic deities identified with Apollo, gods of light and thermal waters, are closely associated in worship and myth with a goddess. We have seen that Grannus's bride is Sirona, the goddess of the stars and rebirth, with ears in her hand and a crescent on her forehead. Borvo's bride is Ritona, the goddess of the fords honored by the Treveri. However, in the territory of the Lingoni in Borvo, an important healing goddess is associated: Damona. Damona's name means "divine cow", perhaps regarding her character as the goddess of fertility. In

Alesia city, she is paired with Apollo Moritasgus. Here, a temple is dedicated to both. Damona is represented there in a stone image; she has spikes on her head and holds a coiled snake in one hand, which perhaps symbolizes rebirth. As the snake sheds its skin and becomes young again, so the pilgrim hopes to recover from his illnesses and return to health. In one of the Damona sanctuaries in this region, there is an incubation room; here, the sick spend the night hoping that the goddess will visit them in a dream and heal them. Also in the territory of the Lingons, Damona is mated with the god Albius, the "White", also a transparent local form of Apollo. Here, there is a votive pit where pilgrims throw ex-votos and other objects in honor of the goddess, especially small statuettes that represent her.

Belenus, the Shining One, is the god of light, assimilated by the Romans to Apollo. He is a young and radiant god. His cult seems to originate in a not-very-large area whose center is around the Eastern Alps. It seems that the Norics adore him as a god of their province; one of his centers of worship is

Aquileia. From here, the cult of Belenus extends southward on the east coast of Cisalpine Gaul. Other ramifications lead instead to southern Gaul, where he is venerated in Nemausius (Nîmes) and Narbonne. One of his temples seems to be in Burdigala (Bordeaux). In Tivoli, the emperor Hadrian could not ask for anything better than to enhance the beauty of his favorite Antinous by comparing it to the splendor of Belenus. Cunobeline, leader of the Trinovanti, seems to have been particularly devoted to him. This is revealed by his very name: "dog of Belenus". It was he who minted coins bearing the image of the god on the front, surrounded by a crown of flaming rays to represent the splendor of the sun, while on the reverse appears the figure of a boar. The Celtic festival of May 1st is dedicated to Belenus.

Maponos, the Divine Son, is a god of the Celts of Britain, especially worshiped by the Brigantes tribe. The god is known, among other things, for his skill in the art of music. Hence, he has been identified with Apollo citharode. The cult of this Divine Son should perhaps be combined with that of a Divine

Mother, called Matrona. In fact, the Celts say that the goddess Latona, mother of Apollo, was born on an island opposite Gaul, and therefore in Britain. And indeed, in Britain, near the city of Verolam (St. Albans in Herefordshire) stands a large and famous circular temple, the Fanum Maponi, which the Celts consecrated to the radiant Divine Son.

Chapter 10: The Cycle Of
Invasion of Ériu

The Story of Tuan: Immortality and Memory

The problem of how the memory of people who disappeared into thin air could be passed on must have fascinated the Irish chroniclers, who came up with various figures of immortals who lived through the centuries perpetuating the stories of their people. I choose the myth of Tuan mac Cairill as a "frame" through which to focus on the Cycle of Invasions.

1.   The Guest of Finnian of Clonard

It is said that one day (we are at the beginning of the 6th century), saint (noíb) Finnian of Clonard left the monastery he founded in the Ulaid and went to find an old warrior who lived not far from there. However, Tuan, son of Cairill, was very rude to the saint, refusing to receive him. Then Finnian sat outside the door of the surly warrior's house and fasted all Sunday. Faced with such obstinacy, Tuan finally welcomed the monk into his home. Good relations were established between the two and Finnian returned to his monks in Ulaid.

"Tuan is an excellent man," he told them. "He will come to you to comfort you and tell the ancient stories of Ériu." In fact, the warrior soon arrived in the monastery and proposed that the monks go with him to his hermitage. The monks followed him and celebrated the Sunday offices, complete with psalms, prayers, and mass. When the monks asked him what his name was and what his lineage was, he gave an astonishing answer:

"I'm a man from Ulaid," he declared. "My name is Tuan, son of Cairill. However, once I was called Tuan, son of Starn, brother of Partholon. This was my name in the beginning." Then Finnian asked Tuan to tell his story and added that none of the monks would accept his food until Tuan had told what he remembered.

So Tuan began to tell.

2.   The Story of Tuan mac Cairill

Tuan told of five invasions which, after the flood, came to occupy Ériu – and, indeed, he never mentioned anyone who had arrived in Ériu before the flood . Three centuries after the flood had reached Ériu, he said, Partholon, son of Sera, had settled there with his people. However, following a plague, in the space of two Sundays, the entirety of the People of Partholon had been annihilated. Now, because it was the law that at least one person could survive every massacre afterward, by divine decision, Tuan had survived the epidemic, the only survivor of all his people. For years, Tuan had wandered alone among the cliffs and hills, guarding himself against wolves, until he was so old that, unable to walk comfortably, he retired to Ulaid, where he found refuge in a cave. For twenty-two years, Tuan had been alone on the empty island of Ériu, until he saw new people land on the island from the top of a hill. It was Nemed, a distant descendant of Partholon himself, who came with his people to colonize the island. Old and miserably naked, with gray hair and long nails, Tuan did not have the courage to meet the new arrivals, so he fled to hide in his cave, where he would await death. However, one night, while Tuan was sleeping, his body changed shape. When he awoke, he found that God had turned him into a deer, restoring his youth and cheerful mood at the same time. And Tuan sang these verses:

- They come to me, sweet Lord,

the Nemedians son of Agnoman;

mighty warriors in battle,

ready to seek my blood.

However, they rise on my head

two stages bristling with sixty points:

new shape, coarse and gray hair

when I was deprived of strength and defense.

And Tuan was prince of the deer of Ériu. Great herds surrounded him no matter what path he followed. He spent this new life of his at the time when Nemed and his descendants inhabited the green Ériu. By the time the Nemedians also disappeared, Tuan, transformed into a deer, had already reached extreme old age. His horns were worn out and his once agile legs could no longer escape the packs of wolves. So Tuan retired to his cave in Ulaid to die. However, one morning, when he woke up, he realized that his body had changed shape again. He had transformed into a black boar. Tuan sang:

- Today boar among the herds,

mighty lord of great triumphs,

I was once among the People of Partholon

in the assembly that regulated the judgments.

My song was pleasant to everyone,

pleasing to young and beautiful women;

I had a majestic and shining chariot,

grave and sweet voice in the long journey;

quick pace, without fear

to combat and assault:

yesterday I had a beautiful and radiant face,

today I'm a black boar!

Young again in this new form, Tuan regained his good humor. He was the king of Ériu's boars and proudly roamed the island. Another people came from the sea to occupy Ériu. They were the Fir Bolg. Meanwhile, Tuan's life had come to an end: The spirit was weary, powerless to do what it was capable of doing before. The old boar lived only in dark caves and between cliffs. Then Tuan returned to his cave in Ulaid, to that same place where he returned every time the load of the years made him fall back into old age, so that his appearance would change and he would find his youth again. This time he came out transformed into a sea hawk. His spirit became happy and he was capable of anything again. He became restless and lively; he flew all over the island and sang these lines:

- Today sea hawk, yesterday boar,

God who loves me

gave me this form.

I lived among the herds of wild boars,

today they are among the flocks of birds.

And then a new people came to take over Ériu. It was the Túatha Dé Danann, who won the Fir Bolg, who at the time occupied the green island. As for Túan, he remained for a long time in the form of a hawk and was still in that appearance when a further invasion arrived: that of the Milesians, who tore the island from the Túatha Dé Danann. Now old, the hawk was in the hollow of a tree above a stream, his spirit struck down, unable to fly. After he fasted for nine days, sleep took hold of him and he was transformed into a river salmon. Later, God placed him in the water, where the salmon lived and was comfortable, vigorous, and well-fed. Skilled in swimming, he escaped dangers and traps: the hands of the fisherman, the talons of the hawk, the fishing lances. One day, God decided it was time to put an end to the state of Tuan and that was how a fisherman ended up catching that big salmon.

3.   Reborn

The salmon was brought to the court of King Cairell, son of Muiredach Muinderg. The salmon was placed on the grill and roasted. The king's wife, as soon as she saw the salmon, was overcome by an irresistible temptation; she wanted it served, and she ate it greedily. Not for this Tuan ceased to be conscious. He kept a memory of the time he remained in the womb of the woman and from there he heard all the conversations that were held in the house, of what was going on in Ériu in those days. Then the queen gave birth and he was born, and was called Tuan again. As soon as he was born, Tuan could speak perfectly and told of the very ancient events he had witnessed. Throughout his life, Tuan mac Cairill had been a prophet until Pátraic came to bring faith in Ériu. Tuan was already very old, but he had been baptized. He was very old now, and this was the story he told Finnian and his monks: the chronicle of the ancient invasions of Ériu.

It is thanks to Tuan mac Cairill that the historians of Ériu still have the memory of Partholon and its people today.

The Creation: The Biblical Tale in the Irish Myth

The Celtic creation myth was never handed down; Christian monks conveniently replaced it with the biblical story. The result is a Genesis full of extra-canonical news, endowed with a bizarre sense of the marvelous and subtly oriented in an "Irish" sense.

1.   The Creation of the World

The world was created, according to the calculation of the most attentive Irish annalists, 5194 years before the birth of our Lord, Christ.

In principio fecit Deus Caeum et Terram...

In the beginning, God made heaven and earth, He who has no beginning and no end. This happened on the fifteenth day of the calends of April, according to the Hebrews and the Latins, although until then the world had never seen either sunrise or sunset. That first Sunday, God made formless matter - fire and air, earth and water - and the light of the angelic hierarchies. On Monday, he made the seven heavens and the firmament. On Tuesday, he made the land and the sea. On Wednesday, he made the sun and the moon and the stars of the sky. On Thursday, he made the birds of the air and the reptiles of the sea.

171

On Friday, he made the beasts of the earth and then created man to govern and administer them. On Saturday, God stopped at the completion of his creation and blessed it. However, that doesn't mean he turned away from governing it. In this way, God made creatures: some with a beginning but without an end, like the angels; others with a beginning and an end, like animals without reason; and still others with a beginning and an end but without an end, like men, who have a beginning when they are born, a term in their mortal bodies, and no term in their immortal souls.

2.   The Heaven on Earth

God made a paradise on earth, in the plain of Arón (which others call Eden), on the southern coast of that land which is located in the east of the world (just as Ériu is in the extreme west of the earth, on the northern side). In paradise is the Pairtech mountain, which the sun illuminates as it rises. Not far away is the source of Nuchal, from which four free and mighty rivers flow. The Pishon is the first river, made of oil, which flows eastwards. The Tigris is the second, of wine, which goes west. The Euphrates is the third, with honey, flowing south. The Gihon is the fourth, made of milk, which heads north.

In the center of paradise, in the plain of Arón, rises the forbidden tree, whose name is Daisia, and which produces many kinds of wonderful fruit.

3.   Adam and Eve

When God created the first man, he did so in this guise: the body of common earth, the head of the earth of Garad, the chest of the earth of Arabia, the belly of the earth of Lodain, and the legs of the earth of Agoria.

Others say that God took the land of the Malón region for the head, the land of Arón for the chest, the land of Babylon for the belly, or that of Byblos, and the land of Laban and Gogoma for the legs. For three days the splendid semblance of Adam remained lifeless, after it had been shaped by the earth. His blood and sweat came from water, his breath from air, his heat from fire, and his soul from the breath of God.

It was on the eastern side of Pairtech, the mountain of heaven, that Adam first stood up and welcomed the rising sun. It was then that he raised a hymn to the Lord. "I adore you, I adore you, oh my God!"

These were the first words that were ever spoken. Adam's body was strong and perfect. He moved, and then ran toward the springs of Paradise. God presented all the animals to Adam so that he could give each one a name.

However, Adam was overcome with great sadness because every animal had a mate and he was alone. Then God made sleep fall upon him, took a rib from him, and created Eve. As soon as the woman was introduced to Adam, he laughed with joy. That was the first laugh.

And Adam said: "Here are the bones of my bones and the flesh of my flesh." And this was the first prophecy that was uttered, as God, when he put Adam to sleep, gave him the gift of prophecy.

4.   The Downfall

God assigned the rule of heaven to Lucifer, with nine orders of angels under his command, and gave the land to Adam and Eve, and their offspring. However, then, blinded by presumption and pride, Lucifer rebelled and attacked heaven, supported by a third of all the celestial hosts.

God struck him down and hurled him and all his angels to Hell, saying: "Arrogant is this Lucifer; so let's go down and confuse his decisions." This was the first judgment that was ever pronounced.

Lucifer had jealousy and hatred toward Adam, to whom God had promised heavenly bliss in his stead.

Using the power that came to him from the ineffable name of God, Lucifer assumed the appearance of a serpent, his body as thin as air, and placed himself in the path of the first man and the first woman.

The snake persuaded the woman and then the man to sin, causing them to eat an apple from the forbidden tree. The reason God forbade eating the fruit of that tree was that if Adam did, he would understand that he was under the power and authority of the Lord.

5.   The Fratricide

At the age of thirty, Adam was created, and Eve looked twenty when God took her from the rib of man. So Adam was only fifteen years old when he fathered Cain and his sister Chalmana. In the thirtieth year of Adam's life, Abel and his sister Delbora were born. One day, Cain and Abel offered two rams to the Lord. However, God did not like Cain's offer, while he accepted Abel's.

Behold, seized by jealousy and pride, Cain brandished a camel's jaw and struck his brother, just as the victims of sacrifices are struck, killing him. Abel's blood stained the stones of the earth, which since then ceased to grow. Some say that it was Seth, seeing the blood of sin, who collected the camel bone, but this is not possible because it was only long after Abel's death, in the hundred and thirtieth year of Adam's life, that Seth was born, from which Adam's posterity would descend. Others say that Cain's hatred of Abel was dictated by jealousy, as they were both in love with Chalmana.

However, Adam, judging the relationship between Cain and his twin too close, had supported Abel's claim against Cain's, provoking the latter's murderous reaction. Others say that Pendan, son of Adam, was later the husband of Chalmana, and this led Cain to a second fratricide.

After the killing of Abel, seven sores appeared on Cain's body: two on the hands, two on the feet, two on the cheeks, and one on the forehead. And it was precisely in the wound on his forehead that Cain, much later, would be hit by the apple thrown by Lamech, thus ending his wretched days.

The ram that Abel had offered to the Lord would later replace Isaac, son of Abraham, on the altar of sacrifice. The same skin would be seen later, when Christ washed the feet of his disciples.

6.   The Age of Patriarchs

After the killing of Abel, God decided to send the flood on the earth to wipe out humanity, who lived in sin. The only one to be saved was Noah, aboard his ark. This is the genealogy of Noah: Noah, son of

Lamech, son of Methuselah, son of Enoch, son of Jared, son of Mahalel, son of Kenan, son of Enos, son of Seth, son of Adam.

There were three sons of Adam who had descendants, but only the lineage of Seth survived the flood, while the race of Cain was wiped out, as was the race of Sile.

According to the Jewish annalists, who summed up the years of the generations of the patriarchs, between the creation of Adam and the flood, one thousand six hundred and fifty-six years passed. This calculation is confirmed by the verses of the ancient poets of Ériu:

The first age of the melodious world

from Adam to the flood,

fifty-six years, clear calculation,

plus six hundred plus a thousand

7.   The Flood

When, indeed, God saw that the people of Seth's clan were transgressing his command, that there was no relationship or alliance with the people of the race of wicked Cain, he decided to send the flood to wipe out mankind. Only Noah had continued to obey the divine command and had avoided joining the clan of Cain. God decided that Noah would be saved with his family and commanded him to prepare an ark so that he could escape the catastrophe.

The ark was made of wood, coated inside and out with bitumen. Thirty cubits was its height, three hundred cubits its length, and fifty cubits its width. The door opened on the eastern side. Noah brought a pair of all unclean animals and three pairs (or seven) of the pure into the ark so that he could dispose of the victims for sacrifice once they had come out of the ark.

Noah had Coba for his wife, who was his sister. He had three children, Shem, Ham, and Japheth, who had married their three sisters. Six hundred years was the age of Noah when he entered the ark. He went aboard, with his family, on the seventeenth day of the May moon, Friday, and God closed the door behind him. It rained continuously for forty days and water covered the earth. The flood engulfed all men and beasts except the eight who were on the ark and the animals that had been loaded into it. (However, the antiquarians remember that Enoch, who was in heaven fighting the Antichrist, and Fintan mac Bóchra, who was locked up in his cave in Ériu, were also saved, as God had chosen him to tell men the stories of the ancient times.) Twelve cubits was the level of the water on the highest mountains and this for an obvious reason: The ark was immersed for ten cubits and emerged for twenty. In this way, the tops of the highest mountains would remain two cubits under the keel of the ark, without damaging it.

After a hundred and fifty days, the waters began to dry up. For seven months and twenty-seven days, the ark was tossed from wave to wave until, finally, it rested on the mountains of Armenia. The waters receded until the tenth month, and on the first day of the tenth month, the tops of the mountains began to be seen. At the end of another forty-seven days, Noah opened the window of the ark and sent out the crow, which never came back. The next day, he let go of the dove, and it returned because it had not found a place to rest. Noah sent out the dove again after seven days, and in the evening the dove returned, carrying an olive branch with leaves in its beak. After another seven days, Noah sent it out again and the dove never came back. Noah came out of the ark on the twenty-seventh day of the May moon, Tuesday, in the six hundred and first year of his life. The first thing he did when he got out of the ark was to raise an altar to God and offer him a sacrifice.

8. The Second Age of the World

The second age of the world began. Noah was the first man to undertake agricultural work in the first year after the flood. He began to plow and reap, and planted a vineyard. His wife Coba was the first to sew clothes for the small community.

Shem, son of Noah, was the first blacksmith, the first craftsman, and the first carpenter after the flood. Japheth was the first to play the harp and organ after the flood. Ham was the first poet and the first bard.

It is said that, before the flood, Ham had erected three four-sided columns, one of lime, one of clay, and one of wax, and had written on them the stories of the antediluvian times to be known after the catastrophe. The lime column and the clay column were destroyed by the flood, but the wax column remained intact: and it was thus that the stories of the time before the flood were passed down and survived into the later ages of the world. Noah divided the world into three parts among his children:

Shem took up residence in pleasant Asia, while Ham went with his children to Africa. The noble Japheth and his offspring settled in Europe.

It is also said that Ham was cursed by Noah, and was enslaved by his two brothers. From him then descended deformed and grotesque lineages, such as the Lupracanaig, the Fomorians, and the horse-headed Gaburchinn, perhaps to be identified with the Pucai. This was the origin of the monsters.

Conclusion

In view of the undeniably mixed character of the populations called "Celtic" at the present day, it is often urged that this designation has no real relation to any ethnological fact. The Celts who fought with Caesar in Gaul and with the English in Ireland are, it is said, no more-they have perished on a thousand battlefields from Alesia to the Boyne, and an older racial stratum has come to the surface in their race. The true Celts, according to this view, are only to be found in the tall, ruddy Highlanders of Perthshire and North-west Scotland, and in a few families of the old ruling race still surviving in Ireland and in Wales. In all this I think it must be admitted that there is a large measure of truth. Yet it must not be forgotten that the descendants of the Megalithic People at the present day are, on the physical side, deeply impregnated with Celtic blood, and on the spiritual with Celtic traditions and ideals. Nor, again, in discussing these questions of race-character and its origin must it ever be assumed that the character of a people can be analysed as one analyses a chemical compound, fixing once for all its constituent parts and determining its future behaviour and destiny. Race-character, potent and enduring though it be, is not a dead thing, cast in an iron mould, and there-after incapable of change and growth. It is part of the living forces of the world; it is plastic and vital; it has hidden potencies which a variety of causes, such as a felicitous cross with a different, but not too different, stock, or in another sphere-the adoption of a new religious or social ideal, may at any time unlock and bring into action.

Lightning Source UK Ltd.
Milton Keynes UK
UKHW021844040722
405350UK00009B/1694

9 781774 856123